Praise for *Prototyping for Designers*

"Prototyping is one of the most important skills for designers to learn and integrate into their practice. When it comes to breaking prototyping into an actionable, teachable framework there is no one more qualified than Kathryn McElroy. This book is an important addition to every designer's bookshelf."

ABBY COVERT, FACULTY, SVA PRODUCTS OF DESIGN

"Prototyping is vital to all stages of product development, from discovering user needs to testing more refined ideas. This book provides an in-depth look at all aspects of the prototyping process. While it's a handy reference for designers and makers, I'd also recommend this book for product managers and design advocates promoting design thinking within their organizations."

CHRIS MILNE, PRODUCT MANAGER AT CAPITAL ONE,
PREVIOUSLY SENIOR DESIGNER/PROTOTYPER AT IDEO

"Prototyping has become an essential way to develop products and services with a focus on the people who will use them. Kathryn McElroy has broken down the fundamentals of prototyping in a clear, accessible, and digestible way that will elevate the skills of designers and nondesigners alike."

DOUG POWELL, DISTINGUISHED DESIGNER, IBM

"Part of being a really great designer is more than being able to have a vision—it is allowing others to see that vision and in turn, changing the way they think. This book is that vision. Kathryn allows the reader to see that prototyping is more than just a check in a checkbox but a mindset that allows you and your designs to grow and succeed. Always be prototyping."

BRENT ARNOLD, CREATIVE DIRECTOR AT MOTIVATE (CITI BIKE), ADJUNCT PROFESSOR AT SVA PRODUCTS OF DESIGN

Prototyping for Designers

Developing the Best Digital and Physical Products

Kathryn McElroy

Beijing · Boston · Farnham · Sebastopol · Tokyo

Prototyping for Designers
by Kathryn McElroy

Published by O'Reilly Media, Inc., 1005 Gravenstein Highway North, Sebastopol, CA 95472.

O'Reilly books may be purchased for educational, business, or sales promotional use. Online editions are also available for most titles (*http://oreilly.com/safari*). For more information, contact our corporate/institutional sales department: (800) 998-9938 or *corporate@oreilly.com*.

Acquisitions Editor: Nicolas Lombardi
Editor: Angela Rufino
Production Editor: Melanie Yarbrough
Copyeditor: Jasmine Kwityn
Proofreader: Molly Ives Brower
Indexer: Lucie Haskins

Cover Designer: Randy Comer
Interior Designers: Ron Bilodeau and Monica Kamsvaag
Illustrator: Rebecca Demarest
Compositor: Melanie Yarbrough

January 2017: First Edition.

Revision History for the First Edition:

2016-12-20   First release

See *http://oreilly.com/catalog/errata.csp?isbn=0636920049487* for release details.

978-1-491-95408-9

[LSI]

In loving memory of my Dad, who always told me you have exactly enough time to do the things that matter most to you. I'm glad I made the time to write this book, and I wish you were here to read it.

[*contents*]

[*Foreword*]

TRUTH BE TOLD, I was completely predisposed to love this book. I don't know anyone who has a more stalwart belief in the value of the proto-type than I do (well, I guess it would be Kathryn McElroy at this point!), and I've lived that devotion in both my professional design practice and in my life as an educator.

Many years ago, I was part of a boutique design consultancy in Norwalk, Connecticut, engaged to imagine "the next toothbrush" for a leading toothbrush manufacturer. We were happy to get the job, but it was clear that other, larger firms were similarly engaged in a kind of "Phase 1" exploration; the company was hedging their bet—not a terrible strat-egy, and pretty common. Instead of having a lot of "brainstorming meetings" and talking about where we might "innovate the next mouth care experience," each of the designers on our team got into the model shop. Back then, we didn't have digital fabrication tools, so everything we created was cut on band saws and table saws, spun on lathes, glued and pinned and lashed together with jerry-rigged joints and fasten-ers, and of course, constructed by hand. We used plastic, wood, metal, cannibalized bristles from other brushes—weird mesh materials and woven fabric samples—really, anything we could get our hands on and be creative with. And we built toothbrushes. Lots of them.

We had only a couple of weeks before the first review with the client, and when they walked into the office they were startled to find some-thing that they were clearly not expecting: a long, long row of physical prototypes—over 100 in all—laid out in a line, with periodic glasses of disinfectant wash. And yes, we had built all of these hacked-together models, and personally tested each by actually brushing with them as we continually prototyped, iterated, and refined them (along with sani-tizing them!), and we expected our clients to do the same. It was one of the most exhilarating presentations we'd ever given—moving through each prototype, sharing everything we'd learned around ergonomics, function, form, fit, color, texture, you name it—and the feedback could not have been more positive. We also found out that the "other design firms" showed the client their spinning animations of high-gloss brush handle renderings on computer screens; they hadn't *made* a thing. (I think you can guess who received the contract to move on to Phase 2.)

During the first year of the Products of Design graduate program I founded at the School of Visual Arts in New York City (and from which Kathryn was one of our inaugural graduates), I made a poster that read, "No Prototype, No Meeting." That poster is still up today, and has become a kind of ethos and rallying cry of the department pedagogy. I wrote that slogan because too often I would pass by small group of students working on a project together...talking. And talking. They were trying to *think* of a (brilliant) idea instead of *building their way* to lots of (generative) ideas. I'd interrupt them and suggest that they each "go make something" independently—even for just half an hour—and then reconvene and respond to what they had made. The results were startling: they always returned with a plethora of ideas, inventions, and new directions, their energy, curiosity, and enthusiasm sky-high. They were happy. And they were on their way to producing truly meaningful work.

In *Prototyping for Designers*, Kathryn McElroy provides a master class in the value of the prototype. But she does many things in addition. Not only does she argue for its value, but she gives us *vocabulary* with which to talk about and distinguish between prototypes, along with methodologies and rationales to help us employ them to their greatest potential impact.

And she does something that I'm not sure even she was expecting: as each of the chapters ladders up in detail and specificity, she deftly builds upon the terms and arguments that she's beautifully laid out in the previous chapters—refining her arguments and building complexity. In a way, of course, she's prototyping her story for us, as she tells it.

And by the end of the book, you're left with a design artifact that is comprehensive, persuasive, and above all, actionable. I can guarantee that you will be able to put what you learn from this book to immediate use tomorrow, and that you will never see the role of prototyping in the same way again. It will become a part of the thinking in your mind, the lexicon in your speech, the habits in your hands, and the excitement in your heart. That sounds like a big deliverable, but this book delivers; in the end, it's no prototype anymore. It's the real thing.

ALLAN CHOCHINOV
FOUNDING CHAIR, MFA PRODUCTS OF DESIGN,
SCHOOL OF VISUAL ARTS; PARTNER, CORE77
NOVEMBER 2016

[*Preface*]

THERE SEEM TO BE hundreds of new smart objects and apps reaching the market every day. With all of this competition, how do you know that your idea will be influential and that people will buy it? If you're familiar with business, you've done some market research and found a viable sector. Or you're working with a team that has an idea and is rushing toward a minimum viable product (MVP). But how can you truly know that your ideal customer will benefit from your new product or app? And how do you know that your team is pursuing the right solution?

Prototyping and user testing is the best way to make valuable products that are impactful for your users. By creating incrementally better prototypes throughout your process, you can get valuable feedback to improve your product. Instead of merely trusting your gut with its assumptions and hidden biases, you can engage with real people to observe how they interact with your prototypes. Through this direct interaction, you'll understand exactly where your users get stuck, what they have trouble grasping, and their visceral reaction to the entire experience. Prototyping is a key to developing a good experience that meets the needs of the end user.

The goal of this book is to give you a foundational education in the topic, providing current examples of companies that prototype, along with best practices and tried-and-true processes. I want to inspire you not only to prototype, but to develop a habit of prototyping. You'll learn how to test your ideas in many ways and gain useful insights to direct you forward. I encourage you to build a culture of prototyping within your team and company. This culture will energize your team to seek feedback in all formats and to help peers give one another supportive, constructive feedback to improve their ideas.

It takes time and effort to learn how to prototype, and nothing will improve your skill more than jumping straight in and making prototypes of your work. This book will help take some of the guesswork out of your initial prototypes, and empower you to find new ways of validating assumptions and ideas.

Why I Wrote This Book

When I started learning product design, I mostly taught myself how to prototype. There wasn't an individual book or obvious online resources to help, just a lot of online tutorials and examples. What I discovered through the limited support I found was that trying, building, and learning was the best way to test ideas. I stumbled through learning by making, slowly creating iterative design updates through getting feedback. This process was painful at times, and I learned a lot by failing.

Some of my failures include prototypes that broke before I could test them, or broke during a testing session with users. From those failures, I learned how robust I needed to make wearable prototypes to withstand testing with real people. Although I treated the prototype gingerly, other people interacted with it more roughly, like they would a real product instead of a hobbled-together early version. For my thesis project, I had to determine which parts of my product idea I needed to build and test, and I made a few versions that weren't helpful in testing early on. Then I figured out that I needed to decide on the assumption I was testing before I made the prototype, to ensure that it would be appropriate and useful.

I want this book to take out some of the hard work of learning prototyping best practices, and inspire you to take action as soon as you have an idea, to try it and test it with real users. There's no substitute for learning by doing, so I'll guide you with insightful best practices and tips, along with many examples of prototypes along the way to help you become comfortable with making prototypes.

You will learn how to prototype and test ideas for physical and digital products. The term *physical product* can cover a huge expanse of product types, but for the purpose of this book I'm focusing on personal electronics with an emphasis on physical computing. Physical computing means "building interactive physical systems by the use of software and hardware that can sense and respond to the analog world." This includes electronics with sensor inputs and some sort of output, including smart objects, wearables, and the Internet of Things (see Figure P-1). It does not include traditional industrial design, which has its own rigorous prototyping practices.

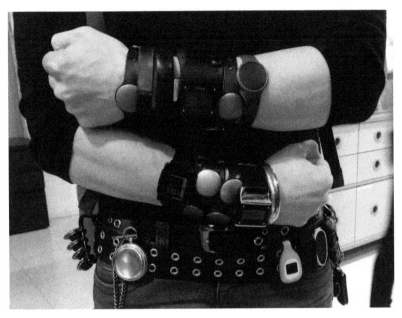

FIGURE P-1

Physical computing products include electronics, smart objects, wearables, and the Internet of Things (photo courtesy of Flickr user doctorow)

Digital products include software and applications that we use on devices that are usually screen-based. This includes smartphone apps, websites, web apps, tablet apps, computer software, and enterprise-level software (see Figure P-2). It likewise includes any platform—from iPhones to Androids, and from Windows PCs to Macs. These digital products can be standalone, or they can be the control interface for a smart object, bringing the physical and digital together into one proto-typing process.

FIGURE P-2

Digital products include apps, websites, computer software, and enterprise-level software (photo courtesy of Wikimedia user Kelluvuus)

At this point in time, these two domains are converging to create multi-modal product experiences, and it's assumed that designers can work across both the digital and physical worlds. This book will widen your horizons by helping you think about both types of products simultaneously. Ubiquitous computing (networks of smart objects that are connected to the internet and to each other) is leading the trend to embed microprocessors into all sorts of products, allowing the objects to talk to each other and use sensors and data to personalize experiences for individual users. Another way to say this is the *Internet of Things*—where each thing has sensors and communicates its data to other smart objects or to a central interface for consumption.

It makes sense to talk about prototyping across both of these mediums in order to connect the often disparate world of electronics and user-centered design. The process of prototyping is similar, and the value of prototyping is high. I'm uniquely qualified to write this book due to my experience building smart objects and wearable electronics and my current work designing enterprise-level software at IBM. By combining these two worlds, you'll be able to step a bit outside your comfort zone in order to try something new in your prototyping practice.

Who Should Read This Book

The ideal reader of this book is someone who's eager to improve their design process. It's geared toward beginning and intermediate designers, and is especially relevant for readers who are shifting careers into product design (either physical or software). However, it applies to many other people.

You might have a DIY project that you think is great, but want to find a way to test it before you invest too much time or money into scaling or selling it. You might be a product designer who knows that you should prototype, but you don't know how to incorporate it into your current workflow or Agile team. You could be interested in user testing and backing up your design decisions with data in order to gain influence with your business stakeholders.

Prototyping is a formalized version of continual learning. Readers with an open mind, and the desire to improve their skill and craft, will benefit the most from this book. I suggest you be as open to improving yourself as you are with improving your product experience.

This book will help you build broad, actionable skills, but it will not include how-tos on specific software. If you're looking for tutorials, there are plenty of online videos with specific lessons on new software. Software comes and goes, and as soon as a book is printed, it's immediately out of date! This book will give you a good foundation in prototyping so that you'll feel comfortable applying it to whichever software you're most comfortable using. Whether that's Adobe Illustrator or Photoshop, Sketch, InVision, or Axure, you'll leave this book with the ability to think through your idea in a way that you can successfully prototype.

How This Book Is Organized

Chapter 1 establishes what prototypes are, with examples from different industries. I discuss product design, including the Agile project management methodology.

Chapter 2 digs into why we prototype. It's not only to test ideas—there are three other major reasons to create prototypes: to understand, to communicate, and to advocate. I'll explain what makes each reason different, and the impact that prototyping has on each.

Chapter 3 is all about fidelity. I cover low to high fidelity, and the five different dimensions of fidelity (visual, breadth, depth, interaction, and data models). I include lots of examples for both physical and digital products so you can start developing the gut instinct you need to choose a fidelity level. This chapter will be a great reference anytime you're not sure how detailed to get with your prototype.

Chapter 4 covers the process of prototyping. I'll start with a minimum viable prototype with generalized steps to break the ice and get you started. Then I'll take you through three different processes to build out prototypes for different situations based on the goal of the prototype. I dig into exploration-based, audience-centric, and assumption-centric processes. To see process in action, I feature a case study with a design team from Etsy, the online handmade marketplace, that demonstrates how prototyping benefited the outcomes of a specific project launch.

Chapter 5 features prototyping for digital products, such as software, apps, and enterprise-level applications. I talk about the unique parts of software design, including animations, responsive design, and designing for accessibility. I then cover low-fidelity paper prototypes to high-fidelity coded prototypes, and discuss best practices that you will be able to apply to any prototyping software you choose. I'll end with a case study from the IBM Mobile Innovation Lab featuring their Stadium experience. This complex project includes prototyping for iPhone, iPad, and large display TVs, and prototyping the immersive experience of attending a football game.

Chapter 6 focuses on how to prototype for physical computing projects. I cover the unique aspects of physical prototyping including materials, electronics, and coding. I will then take you from low-fidelity circuit diagrams to high-fidelity test units with photos and examples. I'll finish up with a case study showing how Richard Clarkson Studio prototypes their ideas in order to improve their products and create new ones.

Chapter 7 teaches you how to user test prototypes to gain impactful insights. I'll show you how to write a research plan and provide examples that you can build from. Then I'll discuss how to find users and conduct the research. Finally, I'll help you synthesize your notes from all the tests to find insights and pain points that need to be improved.

Chapter 8 pulls everything together through a case study from the IBM Mobile Innovation Lab. They created the Tasting Experience, a personalized beer recommendation experience, for SXSW. We'll go through their process of developing and testing their physical user interface (an interactive bar top using visual recognition technology) and their digital barkeeper iPad app and visualization display animations.

Chapter 9 wraps up everything I've covered in the book and challenges you to find a way to prototype for your current project or idea.

By the end of this book, you'll understand how to create the right prototype that you need and at a variety of different fidelity levels. You'll know how to user test your prototypes to get the best insights to improve your product. And you'll feel empowered to take the next step in prototyping for your current project!

Acknowledgments

This book would not be possible without the dedicated support of my family, friends, coworkers, and contributors. Thank you to my husband first and foremost, for putting up with my crazy writing hours and piles of Post-its, and for motivating me to continue and finish this book. Thank you to my parents for raising me to take risks and to share my talents. This book is one small way that I can give back.

Thanks to Allan Chochinov and the MFA Products of Design program and faculty for providing the environment and opportunity to learn by failing, and in turn teaching me how to prototype through trial and error.

Thank you to my O'Reilly editor Angela Rufino for her endless support, and Mary Treseler and Nick Lombardi for giving me the opportunity to speak and write about prototyping for an audience of which I couldn't have dreamed.

Thank you to my steadfast coworkers who inspire me every day at IBM. Thanks especially to my coworkers who contributed case studies, stories, or images, including Aaron Kettle, Aide Gutierrez-Gonzalez, Sushi Sutasirisap, Greg Effrein, and Paul Roth.

Thank you to everyone who contributed their thoughts and personal prototyping processes through conversations and interviews, especially Randy Hunt, Alex Wright, Chris Milne, and Lisa Woods, and those who extensively shared of their work through case studies, including Richard and Erin Clarkson and Kuan Luo.

[1]

What Is a Prototype?

In THIS CHAPTER, I'LL share current views on what makes a prototype and how to prototype in your everyday work.

Everything Is a Prototype

Each thing that you make or activity that you do can be improved. Nothing is ever completely finished; you simply run out of time for the current release. Even if you're happy with the product you deliver, your users will have feedback, and there are bound to be tweaks and changes that you need to make for future versions or releases. No matter how many times you test or prototype, you will always be able to find something new to improve in your product.

The Oxford definition of a prototype is: "A first, typical or preliminary model of something, especially a machine, from which other forms are developed or copied."[1] The word originates from the Greek *prōtotupos*, meaning "first example." By this definition, anything that takes an idea out of your head and makes it visible to others may be considered a prototype. The critical element that this definition is missing is the intention to test and improve the prototype over time. So our definition of a prototype moving forward is: a manifestation of an idea into a format that communicates the idea to others or is tested with users, with the intention to improve that idea over time. If you prefer a more specific definition of prototyping, this book will still be useful. However, I ask you to keep an open mind to what prototyping might be, and how you might incorporate this skill into all areas of your work and life.

---

1 "Prototype—Definition of Prototype in English | Oxford Dictionaries," Accessed March 09, 2016, *https://en.oxforddictionaries.com/definition/us/prototype*.

This broad definition allows you to think about how you can prototype any kind of idea in your life. You might sketch a floor plan before you move into a new house or try out a few different furniture arrangements before finalizing how to set up your living room (Figure 1-1). You can write out a recipe to test, and update the ingredients depending on how the results tasted. Or you might write out your goals to communicate them to others and to remind yourself as you work toward them and update them as you go. This book is even a prototype because the technologies and prototyping methods will continue to evolve after this book is published. Future releases of this book will be improved based on reader feedback and new programs that come out. Each of these examples is a model of an idea, in a format that can be tested and improved.

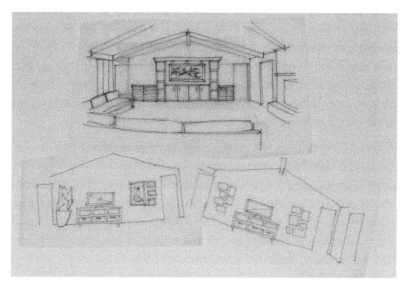

FIGURE 1-1

Drawing alternative furniture layouts is a prototype for decorating your house

Each person you interact with has her own preconceived notion of what a prototype is. Even you have a base understanding of what you think a prototype must be. A developer might believe a prototype has to be made in code, and that it will eventually be used as production code. Designers might think prototypes are clickable mock-ups that they create in programs like InVision or Sketch. Business stakeholders might think a prototype is a proof of concept (POC) that is fully functional and can be used by their sales team for client demonstrations. At its fundamental core, a prototype can simulate a behavior or experience without even needing a representation of its tangible embodiment. Each of these ideas is a valid but limited view on what a prototype can be.

Experienced designers take a broader approach to defining what a prototype is. Randy Hunt, VP of Design at Etsy, equates prototyping with "auditioning," after seeing a film set production team "audition" different physical objects to try them in the background of a scene. An audition allows you to see how the scene, or product, might look in context, and test the object with the real characters and interactions before it's forever captured on film. It's an elegant way to think about your product as an actor in the user's life. Try out a few different acting styles and characters before settling on the right fit for the scene you're designing (Figure 1-2).

FIGURE 1-2
Arranging a set is one way to audition the different objects in your scene (photo courtesy of Flickr user prayitnophotography)

Chris Milne, prototyper for IDEO, calls prototyping an interview, where the idea must impress you with its application. Or the prototype's function must impress users when they interact with it. By prototyping, you're allowing your ideas to interact with your users in a safe place. Let them interrogate each other; learn from the way the two click or don't click. Take feedback from those sessions and design a better candidate for your user to interview again. This broad viewpoint gives you the incentive to improve the aspects you have control over—the product design, interface, experience, and feel—so that users can find the right fit for their need. You might not be able to control where users interact with your product (on a busy sidewalk or in the quiet of their home), but you'll have created an intuitive product that they'll want to use.

These broader definitions allow us to apply prototyping to many stages of product development, and to expand the scope of what a prototype can be. *Scope* means the "extent of the area or subject matter that something deals with or to which it is relevant."[2] When you expand the scope of what you prototype, you're creating more opportunity areas to test and get feedback. The previous, more specific types of prototypes are each useful at different stages of product development. However, you should consider all of the facets of prototyping before choosing which one is appropriate for your current situation. When you approach prototyping for improving and testing your idea, keep in mind your teammates' and stakeholders' expectations for this process, and be ready to explain why you're prototyping in different ways at every stage. You will be the advocate for prototyping throughout your process, instead of only once or in one specific way. This book will give you confidence so you can stand up for the value of prototyping.

What is considered a prototype is often a debated topic for designers, too. The main conflict arises between interactive and static prototypes. Some designers believe a prototype is anything that is testable and improvable, while others believe a prototype is specifically an interactive version of an idea (Figure 1-3). These two viewpoints are individually valid, but the latter limits how you can test your ideas. If you choose to see everything as a prototype, interactive or static, and use it as an opportunity to test your assumptions through any means possible, you will develop the mindset of incremental improvement and constant feedback that will greatly benefit your product.

---

2 "Definition of Scope in English," *Oxford Dictionaries*, accessed March 10, 2016, *https:// en.oxforddictionaries.com/definition/scope.*

FIGURE 1-3

Static versus interactive prototypes

Prototyping as a Mindset

Prototyping is not a checkbox that you complete once on the way to finishing a project. It is a mindset where you are comfortable with testing unfinished ideas in order to make the best result possible. It's embracing the unknown, and testing ideas early and often. It may feel uncomfortable at first to show ugly, unfinished work. I know that when I started testing early prototypes, I felt apprehensive that my work would be judged or deemed unfit to interact with. I would cringe when users struggled to get through the task I set out for them.

Showing unfinished work may feel like it goes against your grain and nature—you may like to display finished, polished, perfect designs. To be successful, you must build comfort with vulnerability and be open to feedback. As you start getting more feedback and incorporating it into your designs, you'll see the longer-term benefit in the success of your projects. After a while, you'll thirst for feedback from your users and colleagues. Unfinished work will be hung up all over your workspace with impromptu conversations and formal critique sessions. Each interaction with your work will improve and strengthen your idea and design.

To get the most out of prototyping, you must incorporate it into every part of your process, and constantly be looking for feedback. Show your user flows to your business stakeholders to get their perspective that you're pursuing the proper use cases. Share your wireframes or electrical circuit diagrams with your coworkers to get their critique on the design. User test low- to high-fidelity prototypes with end users to test usability. Everything can be prototyped, and everything is a prototype. There can always be a better, improved version of what you are creating, and it takes time and practice to develop that urge to always be prototyping.

The more comfortable you feel in this mindset, as you practice it, the more likely you'll bring prototyping to the table with your own team. And when your team experiences prototyping and the informed, tested results you deliver, they'll be more likely to push to create more time for this practice. Soon your business partners and developer colleagues will be asking to see and experience your prototypes and expect it to be part of the project process. Your prototyping and research may even help inform your team's launch dates and prioritize your backlog of future features. As your prototyping skills become stronger and you develop the ability to quickly build prototypes, you'll soon be able to conduct more rounds of testing and ensure your users will get the best product possible.

Prototype Examples

All sorts of industries create prototypes of their work to test and incrementally improve their ideas. I'll talk about two analogous examples and the two main industries that we'll cover in the rest of the book. Prototypes can benefit any industry and field by creating early drafts of work that can be refined and improved before they're finished.

ARCHITECTURE

Architects must develop complex systems that include building programs (what it's being used for), circulation, structural integrity, material choice, heating and cooling systems, mechanical and electrical systems, plumbing, and airflow. They design the whole experience of a building by incrementally improving all of these aspects through drawing, modeling, and testing. Some of their prototypes include floor plans (which are drawn and redrawn based on user input and needs), airflow models (testing ventilation throughout a space by showing how air will move through the rooms), daylight models (improving window design by testing how much light they let in at any point in the day or year), material studies, and aesthetic models (Figure 1-4). More complex models include simulated walk-throughs to test the interior feeling and experience of spaces both on screen and in virtual reality. One architectural firm in Norway creates full-scale floor plans of their designs to allow clients to literally walk through the space and understand the layout and flow of the space.[3]

Each of these prototypes has a specific use and improves the building based on the testing of the models. Using prototypes allows architects to communicate design decisions with clients at different stages to get approval and to communicate final specifications to contractors and engineers for them to build on site. I have firsthand experience with how architecture relates to product design because of my undergraduate degree in architecture. I learned how to create models and presentations to communicate my design intents for a building or space. Much of my architectural training has come in handy as I draw blueprints for digital products and build electronics people interact with.

FIGURE 1-4
Architects create models and prototypes that are used to test floor plans, airflow, daylight, and materials (photo courtesy of Flickr user eager)

---

3 Kurt Kohlstedt, "One to One: Full-Scale Floor Plans Help Architects Walk Clients Through Design," 99% Invisible, *http://bit.ly/2gQ9163*.

INDUSTRIAL DESIGN

Industrial designers have a strong practice in creating huge quantities of prototypes. As they design new shapes and forms for their physical products, they test along the way to make sure their designs are ergonomic and easy to use, and that the forms they design are manufacturable (Figure 1-5). They think about the different ways to design products through both sketches and physical models.

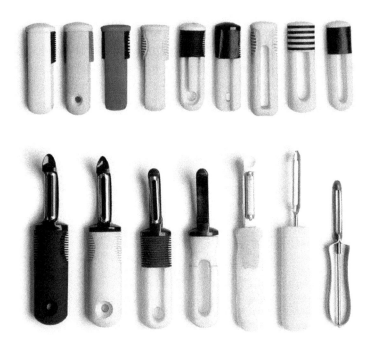

FIGURE 1-5

Shape models for the OXO Good Grips Swivel Peeler (photo courtesy of OXO)

Some of their prototypes include a plethora of sketches, foam models, material studies, aesthetic models, scaled mock-ups, and final forms (Figure 1-6). Once they decide on a general form, they build it in the proper materials and test it for material longevity and ergonomics using academic standards, before finalizing and preparing it for manufacturing. Industrial designers spend most of their time prototyping and testing their ideas before deciding on the final form for production. They then use the prototypes to communicate final design decisions to manufacturers. Prototypes are invaluable to the industrial design process.

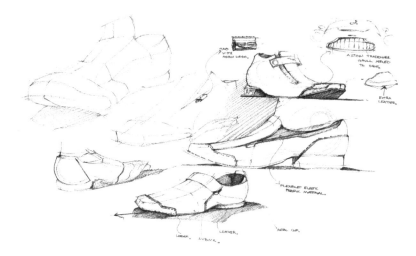

FIGURE 1-6

Industrial designers sketch and prototype prodigiously before choosing the proper, final form for their specific use case (photo courtesy of Flickr user Kirby)

PERSONAL ELECTRONICS

When developing personal electronics, a subset of industrial design, designers begin with sketches and studies of form. Additionally, they deal with layers of complexity, including choosing and testing the necessary electrical components and combining them together until the whole system works. The decisions they make about which components to use have wider implications for the form factor and layout of the final device.

For their purpose, they break down the system into testable pieces, building prototypes with larger electrical components first, then slowly combine them together to get the code to work properly to incorporate the full functionality (Figure 1-7). It is not until after the components are working well together that these designers start using smaller versions of the components and user testing them in the actual final setting (Figure 1-8). This type of product design requires material testing and a parallel process of prototyping an accompanying app, if necessary, that will control the device. We'll delve deeply into the process of electronics prototyping in Chapter 6.

FIGURE 1-7

Personal electronics and wearable products require detailed prototypes to test components, interactions, and final materials

FIGURE 1-8
Once the individual
pieces are assembled,
a more complex
prototype can test user
interactions

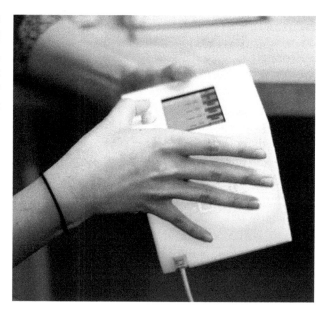

SOFTWARE AND APPS

Software designers create prototypes to fully think through how users will interact and find their way through complex interfaces. These prototypes include user flows to show an ideal user path and to determine the functionality that the user will need; wireframes in a testable form (either paper or clickable); coded prototypes; and visually designed, high-fidelity prototypes (Figure 1-9). Early on, designers explore multiple ways to solve the same problem, testing them with users to determine the ideal path forward. Each of these prototypes incrementally gets better, and allows the designer to improve the overall interactions with the software throughout the process based on testing.

Each software prototype has a specific use and assumption or question that it tests. Earlier in a process, prototypes target big-picture questions like how the information architecture (the structural design and organization of software and websites) should be organized, overall user flows, and the format of the product. Later on in the process, prototypes are more refined to test specific elements such as styles, interaction patterns, and UI text. Designers use prototypes to communicate interactions and to define behavior and functionality to their development teams who implement (or carry out) the designs in code. Being able to see the animations and high-fidelity visuals helps developers give feedback on feasibility, scope their work, and deliver the final product.

FIGURE 1-9

Digital software and apps need initial paper prototypes, clickable prototypes, and high-fidelity prototypes to develop intricate interactions (image courtesy of Flickr user Johan Larsson)

Prototyping for Products

Many of the prototyping examples thus far are a form of product development, but there's more to it than inventing a new thing to sell. Product development encompasses many processes for bringing a new product, service, or experience to market and includes business strategy, market research, value propositions, technical specifications, sales, design, and development (Figure 1-10).

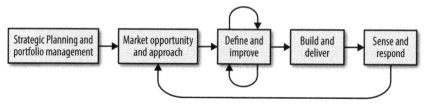

FIGURE 1-10
The product development process

I highly recommend including design in early strategy sessions. By leveraging the design team's user research about the ideal users, business stakeholders can better inform their product strategy (how to solve for a need and prioritize functions) and roadmap (the future plan for implementing additional improvements). For more information on business strategy, check out *UX Strategy* by Jaime Levy or the *Lean Startup* series of books (O'Reilly).

If done well, this combined process will result in happy, satisfied customers. But often in companies, the initial stages and market research are performed solely by a business stakeholder or the engineer who invented the solution. Design can be left out of many foundational decisions, and only included in a small portion of the development cycle.

What if your business stakeholders don't currently include designers in their strategy? How can you gain a seat at the table? The best way to get included is to show the benefits of the additional design research and work without being asked. Your business stakeholders might not realize the value of user research and prototyping, and they won't be able to ask for something they don't know about.

Try incorporating research insights into your regular presentations. Supply both an insight and recommendations on how to resolve it, so that you're creating positive momentum instead of negative blocking

(Figure 1-11). Don't stand in the way of the team and say "no." Provide real reasons that are user-centered and help point your team in the right direction.

As your business and development teams see the value of your research insights and recommendations, they will begin to ask for it earlier in the process, and use it to inform their decisions. It's a slow process, but very worth it when you're working at an established company that you're passionate about.

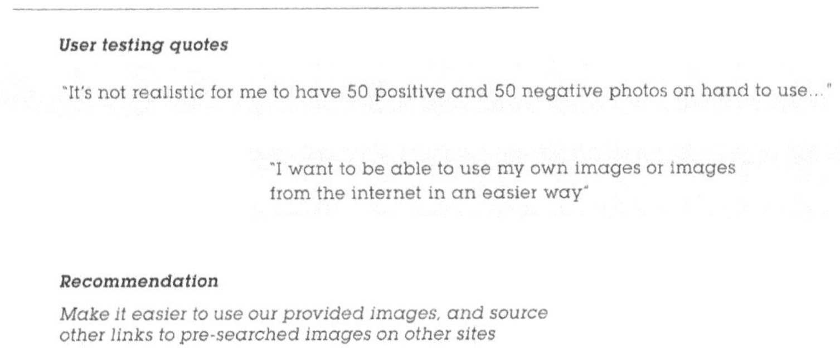

User testing quotes

"It's not realistic for me to have 50 positive and 50 negative photos on hand to use..."

"I want to be able to use my own images or images from the internet in an easier way"

Recommendation

Make it easier to use our provided images, and source other links to pre-searched images on other sites

FIGURE 1-11
Present your research insights with a recommendation for next steps

By interviewing ideal users and testing high-level prototypes with them, designers can give valuable insight into what product direction would best solve the user's problem. This work can help clarify the best direction forward for business stakeholders. It can merge into an Agile development process by working closely with the developers who will code the final digital product or industrial designers who are creating the final forms and manufacturing specs. Agile allows teams to move quickly, test ideas (through various forms of prototypes or MVPs), and fail fast or learn fast as they improve the product (read more about Agile in the sidebar at the end of this chapter).

For example, an API (application program interface for developers) I worked on had a specific way to customize and train the output. After testing a few different interfaces for this training, we heard from many users that they didn't understand why it had to be trained that specific way. They wanted an easier, simpler way to train the API. When we shared this feedback with the engineering team who built the algorithm, they changed their training strategy to better fit the users, and shipped it with the next release, three months later. Due to the updated training, we received plenty of feedback from happy developers who were able to train their specific output faster and more easily. And our paying users increased by three times in the next full month.

This product development framework and prototyping process has been proven countless times by large, established businesses, designers, and successful startups. One historic example is the prolific prototypes that Charles and Ray Eames created for each of their designs (Figure 1-12). They would test many ways of using different materials, fitting to the human form, manufacturing, and finishing. They believed that anyone can create a dream chair in their head, but only by doing the hard work of manifesting that idea into prototypes and then products could they actually fulfill that dream.

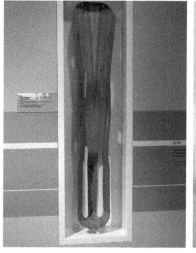 

FIGURE 1-12
Charles and Ray Eames created all sorts of prototypes of their work and built on their explorations into bent plywood (photos courtesy of Flickr users René Spitz and Hiart, respectively)

A Bit About Agile

Agile is a project management methodology of continuous delivery and radical collaboration for software development. Its manifesto is to value:

- Individuals and interactions over processes and tools
- Working software over comprehensive documentation
- Customer collaboration over contract negotiation
- Responding to change over following a plan

This differs from a more traditional project management style called "waterfall" in a few specific ways. Waterfall is more linear, with a specific sequence and handoff of deliverables for each step. The planning phase must be complete before design begins; then design must be complete before it's handed off to developers to implement.

Agile is a more iterative, team-based approach to development that uses time-boxed "sprints" to deliver fully functional components within shorter periods of time. The team starts with an MVP of the product, delivers a fully functional version, then in the next sprint adds the next layer of features to improve the product. Each sprint has a set length, usually in weeks, and at the end of each sprint, the work is delivered and reviewed. Sprints allow for the work to be more flexible, pivoting based on testing results or technology constraints or reprioritizing new features based on market reactions.

Both types of project management have their benefits and downsides, but most software development teams are moving to a more Agile-based approach to allow them to quickly iterate and improve their products without needing to rework a long-term plan. Agile also employs a few "rituals" or "ceremonies" that help teams move quickly, including sprint planning, daily stand-ups, reviews, and retrospectives. Sprint planning and daily stand-ups (short meetings where the team members state what they did the previous day and what they're doing today) keep the team aligned so that each member knows what the other is working on any given day, and what their goal is to complete by the end of the sprint. At the end of a sprint, the team reviews the work that was completed, and performs a retrospective to see if there's anything they can improve for the next sprint.

So where does prototyping fit into this process? Designers break their work down into smaller chunks that can be assigned during specific sprints, such as creating wireframes, making a prototype, testing a prototype, or completing high-fidelity visual design work. For my team specifically, I try to work a sprint ahead of development, so that I can create and test my designs and they're ready to be coded by developers in the next sprint. Part of your design sprint should include prototyping and testing, so make sure to include it as a task when your team does sprint planning. Design tasks should be taken into account for the overall team's planning, and prototyping is no different. Advocate for the time if it's not already on the docket for sprint planning.

For more information on how to incorporate user experience design into Agile practices, check out these resources:

- Doing UX in an Agile World: Case Study Findings (*https://www.nngroup.com/articles/doing-ux-agile-world/*)

- 12 Best Practices for UX in an Agile Environment (*https://articles.uie.com/best_practices/* and *https://articles.uie.com/best_practices_part2/*)

Summary

Prototyping is a mindset of continuous learning that you need to cultivate in yourself and in your team. A prototype can be anything that takes an idea from your head and makes it visible to others or testable with users. As long as you have the intent to improve your prototype, you can't really go wrong with what you build. Prototyping and testing is a common practice in many fields, including architecture, industrial design, personal electronics design, and software design.

Prototyping benefits product development by making sure you're solving the right problem and working in a viable section of the market. All aspects of the product development cycle can benefit from prototyping and designer input. It might take some effort to have your design work valued by business stakeholders earlier in their process. But it's valuable to the longer-term development of the product to have user-centered information in addition to market research numbers.

[2]

Why We Prototype

THERE ARE MANY GREAT reasons to make prototypes and to include them early and often in your process, and the four main points I'll cover are as follows: to understand, to communicate, to test and improve, and to advocate. Each of these is similar, but has a unique twist to why prototypes are valuable and why you should include them at different parts of your design process.

To Understand

Prototyping is a great way to not only understand the problem you're currently trying to solve, but to illuminate alternative problems you should solve instead. This process is called *problem discovery*, and it can help you find the root cause of your user's pain, which might be different than your originally assumed user problem. It's helpful to do problem discovery, through exploratory research and prototyping, early in your process because the further along you are in development, the more difficult and expensive (in time and money) it will be to change directions (Figure 2-1). You will find it easier to pivot as early as you can so that you're on the right track for the product.

FIGURE 2-1

Problem discovery and exploratory research can help define the direction of your project

For example, Segway saw an opportunity area between pedestrian walking and car driving, but didn't spend adequate time researching and validating their problem space (Figure 2-2). They decided to address this problem with a stand-upon solution, but when it hit the market, there were too many assumptions they had already made that were not true, including: access to usable infrastructure, non-rainy climates, no need for multiple passengers, and viability at their price point. If they had done initial research and prototyping with real users, they could have pivoted to an alternative problem and really hit the solution out of the park.

FIGURE 2-2
Segway failed to validate their problem early enough to fix their product design

ALTERNATIVE SOLUTIONS

In addition to understanding the problem, you can explore and understand lots of different ways to solve the problem through drawing and prototyping. It's easy to get stuck in your head thinking about a single solution you've decided to pursue. Early on, you should try out as many variations that you can think of, instead of sticking with your first original idea (Figure 2-3). The best way to explore is to make quick prototypes of all the different ways to solve the user's problem. Then you can conduct task-based tests or A/B tests to compare two or more versions of the same interaction to see which one performs better. Having a user interact with your idea will give you valuable support or invalidation for your current solution or current definition of the problem. You can then move forward with more confidence in your idea and choice of direction.

FIGURE 2-3
Explore many ways to solve your problem

For instance, as illustrated in Figure 2-4, there are many ways to lay out a navigation system for digital products. For a mobile app, you can put it in a tab row at the top or bottom of the screen, or hidden in a hamburger menu (a style of hidden menu that employs an icon of three horizontal lines to indicate menu items will appear when clicked). Or you can display it at the top of the screen and have it scroll away, or have it stay in place as a sticky nav (a persistent or fixed navigation bar that remains at the top of the display window even as you scroll). You might believe that the hamburger menu is the best way for this product layout, but your user might not open that menu, and thus would never find the option within. Although you might have a gut instinct on which direction to go, try testing the different options to see if there's a more intuitive way for your user to navigate your app.

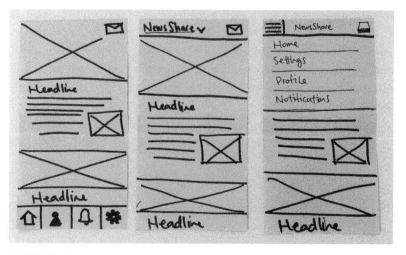

FIGURE 2-4

By testing a few different navigation options, you'll determine which style is best suited for your users

UNDERSTANDING STRATEGY

You can use prototyping to understand your product strategy (as discussed in Chapter 1) through the competitive landscape, direction of the portfolio of products, and the goals of your user. Any artifact that manifests your business direction into a tangible object to share, discuss, and improve will be helpful in defining your product. For example, the Lean Business Canvas (Figure 2-5) will help you articulate the different aspects of your strategy and figure out which areas have risk, questions, and assumptions that you'll need to test. The canvas is a blank template that helps you build a business model by understanding your product and the market it will sell in. You fill out the canvas with the problem you're solving, solution, cost structure, unique value proposition, and key metrics to understand the product side. Then you add the advantage, customer segmentation, revenue streams, and channels to get to customers to understand your market. This one document allows you to communicate your strategy or understand your product manager's strategy for the direction of the product. For a more in-depth look at the Lean Business Canvas, check out *Running Lean* by Ash Maurya (O'Reilly).

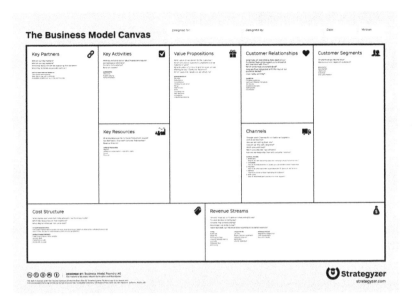

FIGURE 2-5

A Lean Business Canvas will help you prioritize the risks for a new product idea (image courtesy of Wikimedia user Business Model Alchemist)

You can define and test a longer-term product roadmap to understand what will be delivered with each software release or physical product launch. A roadmap describes the next year of work in smaller, prioritized chunks (Figure 2-6). You can reference it to understand what you should be working on next, and what's coming down the pipeline for future work. It's helpful as a tool for the whole team to keep an eye on long-term goals, and for design to be able to validate the direction as you go. Roadmaps are living documents, and need to be revisited often to update and reprioritize based on the work and feedback from users. Make sure you're taking the time to look at both the near and long-term direction of your projects.

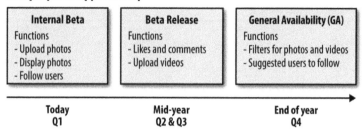

Sample photo app roadmap

Internal Beta	Beta Release	General Availability (GA)
Functions - Upload photos - Display photos - Follow users	Functions - Likes and comments - Upload videos	Functions - Filters for photos and videos - Suggested users to follow

| Today
Q1 | Mid-year
Q2 & Q3 | End of year
Q4 |

FIGURE 2-6

A business roadmap describes the prioritized future steps for a project for the next 6 to 12 months

UNDERSTANDING USER FLOWS

Later on in your process, prototypes help you understand your entire user flow and what you'll need to design for each step of the way. They will help you define the user experience (UX) and design the right user interface (UI), including interactive elements and content. You'll discover new aspects of the design as you draw out each part and think through what the user needs to accomplish their goal. Understanding is a foundational part of your prototyping process, and helpful to conduct throughout any stage of each project.

USER-CENTERED DESIGN

As we move through this book, I'll be talking a lot about users. User-centered design "is the process of designing a tool from the perspective of how it will be understood and used by a human user...rather than requiring users to adapt their attitudes and behaviors in order to learn and use a system."[1] The best way to create a valuable product is to have an initial understanding of who your user is through research, and to engage that potential user throughout your process by testing your prototypes with them to get their feedback. I'll talk more about this prototyping process in Chapter 4 and testing process in Chapter 7.

The first part of user-centered design is fully understanding your user. What specific user or customer will interact with or buy your product? If you answered "everyone" or "me" then your product is not going to

---

1 "Introduction to User-Centered Design," Usability First , Accessed March 9, 2016, *http://www.usabilityfirst.com/about-usability/introduction-to-user-centered-design/*.

speak to anyone specifically in the market, which is a problem. When you leave this question broadly answered, or not answered at all, you will quickly see that users can tell that your product is not designed for them. Even if you are a user of your potential product, you're not the only type of person who will interact with it, and other users don't have your exact same mental model, or thought process. It's vital to get additional points of view on a project, especially when you've been working on it a long time and don't realize your own biases anymore.

To learn about your ideal users you need to build empathy with them; start by talking with them directly to learn about their habits, likes, and dislikes. Demographic information might be helpful, but could taint your understanding with assumptions and unconscious bias. This information typically includes age range, economic status, income level, and education level. Instead, get to know who they are as unique individuals. What is the problem you're solving for them? Don't ask them what you should solve; ask them about any difficulty they have with their workflow. Learn how they currently tackle this problem and what pain points (real or perceived problems) are present in order to discover opportunities for which to design. Ask them about their daily lives—what's their favorite app, what books do they read, what TV shows do they watch, or what activities do they do? These nuances will help you understand who you're designing for, and how to improve their lives.

You can use this research to form *user personas*, which are fictional characters created to represent the different user types that might use a site, brand, or product in a similar way.[2] These personas are snapshots of a user's typical behavior, goals, skills, and attitudes. As a living artifact, continually being informed and updated by research, they help designers and their teammates keep the user at the forefront of their minds when making product design decisions.

If you don't have research about your users, start with an *empathy map* to put yourself in their shoes. An empathy map makes you think about what your users think, feel, say, and do, and can allow you to find hidden pain points and gain a better understanding of your users (Figure 2-7). For a deeper diver into empathy maps and how to create them,

---

2   Wikipedia, "Persona (user experience)," *http://bit.ly/2gQbq7D*.

check out this Cooper article (*http://bit.ly/2gPAT14*) detailing the activities and how to turn an empathy map into a persona. Follow up this activity with interviews of real users to support any insights that you've found.

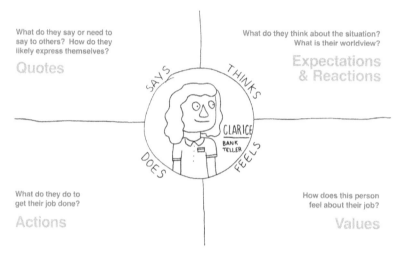

FIGURE 2-7

Empathy maps help you better understand your users and put yourself in their shoes

The best way to figure out what problem a user has is to observe how they deal with the problem currently. Based on your research and interviews, you can create an *As-Is journey map* to determine what their current pain points are. An As-Is journey map goes step by step through the user's current experience, and states what the user is doing, thinking, and feeling throughout the process (Figure 2-8). Once you have the journey mapped, you can pull out the areas that are not ideal, and create solutions to these issues in your product and prototype. Once you find pain points in the journey map, you can prioritize which ones are the most significant to the overall experience, and use that prioritization to guide your prototyping process. For a step-by-step description of how to create an As-Is journey, check out this article by UX for the Masses (*http://bit.ly/2gPEMmB*).

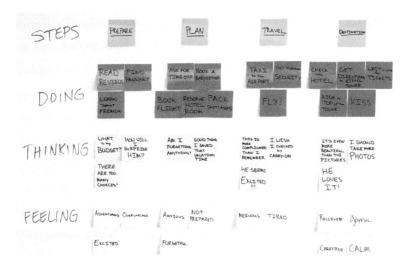

FIGURE 2-8

An As-Is journey map helps you understand the current situation and pain points that you can solve with your product

Since you're not your only user, many of your design decisions will actually be assumptions. An assumption is "a belief or feeling that something is true or that something will happen, although there is no proof."[3] It may be hard at first to recognize what assumptions you've created. For each decision you make, ask yourself if there is evidence to back it, or if it's your gut feeling. You can then reform that assumption into a question that needs to be answered by your user or by additional research.

Testing prototypes will answer many of these questions by providing you proof that either supports or invalidates your assumptions. When you address each of your assumptions, you will have more confidence in your idea and design. You'll know if your user can find their way, complete their goals, and be happy with your product.

By designing for a specific user, keeping a specific user pain point or problem at the center of your product idea and design, you are more likely to find a spot in the market, and an eager customer.

---

3   Oxford Learner's Dictionaries, Definition of assumption (*http://bit.ly/2gQay2D*).

To Communicate

Prototypes make the ideas in your head visible to other people, including the rest of your team, your stakeholders, and your users. They are powerful communication tools if used properly. A prototype articulates your thoughts into a physical or digital medium, and transforms fuzzy, generalized thoughts into a concrete object. If you don't have a prototype, each person you talk with will use their own unique mental model to visualize your idea, and it will be difficult to align all of the different expectations. Instead of talking in vague, general terms, you can point directly to the object or screen you have created and have everyone on the same page in less time.

It's very helpful to have a prototype for each meeting you attend; it centers the conversation on the work instead of on the group's assumptions about the work (Figure 2-9). It will even make your meetings shorter and more to the point, because you will have automatic focus on the exact part of the work you're sharing.

FIGURE 2-9
Prototypes help keep meetings focused and on task

When using a prototyping to communicate, you need to understand who is in your audience and your goal for communicating with them. The prototype you make will be different if you're presenting to a business stakeholder or investor than if you're showing it to fellow designers, because your goal for each meeting will be different. Closing a contract or getting design critiques warrants a specific type of presentation, and potentially, prototype. Your audience will inform what content to include in the prototype, and how you present it. You might frame a presentation as a user story, walking the audience through the use of the prototype by a real end user. Or you might show a small part of an interaction you've designed to communicate with a developer about how you'd like the final interface to look and act.

You'll need to choose your fidelity wisely, dependent on the audience and goal. Fidelity is how closely the prototype resembles the final product. (I'll go in-depth about fidelity in Chapter 3.) If you're talking with other designers, you can use any of the fidelities, keeping in mind what part of the process you're in and what you're communicating or want feedback on. Make sure to give the proper context in a preamble before asking for feedback, in order to direct the conversation in the best way.

For example, if you're presenting your idea for a design critique, you might begin with "this prototype has a higher visual fidelity, but we're still pretty early in the process, so the feedback I'm interested in is if the user flow and the calls to action are intuitive and apparent enough." Now instead of giving you visual design feedback ("there needs to be more whitespace here") your audience of designers can focus on the calls to action ("this button placement is not where I would expect").

Your fellow designers can understand the thoughts and concepts behind a low-fidelity prototype (that doesn't look much like the final version) and can help you think of alternative ways to solve your interaction problems. These early concepts may be as simple as sketches or paper prototypes. You can use mid- or high-fidelity prototypes to get feedback from your colleagues about the visual design and more intricate interactions later in the process (Figure 2-10). It's helpful to have continual check-in meetings with other designers to help you think of different ways to approach the problem and solution, and to give you a set of fresh eyes on your current work. It's especially necessary later in your process when you know your design and subject matter too well, and are blinded to potential alternative design directions.

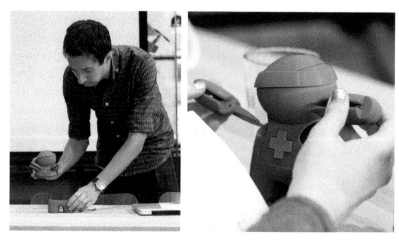

FIGURE 2-10
You can present prototypes for communication in low-, mid-, or high-fidelity

If you're meeting with stakeholders, you need to appropriately show where you are in the process and set proper expectations for the work you will share. You want to underpromise and overdeliver with your work overall, but your audience needs to understand your concepts without thinking they're completely finished. Low-fidelity work is appropriate to get early alignment and approval of user flows, use cases, and features. Once you're designing the solution, either interface or device, a low fidelity may cause your stakeholders to not take your work seriously or understand the concepts you're presenting. If the fidelity is too high, they might assume the work is done and they're seeing a final product. If they believe a product is finished, they won't give you proper feedback and you might leave the meeting without finding alignment. Your best bet for most presentations is to stick with a mid- or mixed-fidelity prototype or provide a few different assets to show the lower fidelity wireframes with a style tile to show the direction of the visual or material design.

If you're communicating with developers or manufacturers who will produce your product, it's best to have a high-fidelity prototype to show exactly how the final product should look and act. Some developers will want *redlines* (annotations that show size and spacing in an interface) and detailed explanations of animations (Figure 2-11). Manufacturers might need specs on the dimensions, materials, and components you've chosen. Your high-fidelity prototype might not be fully functional, but you will need to decide what you want to communicate in order to properly scope the prototype work.

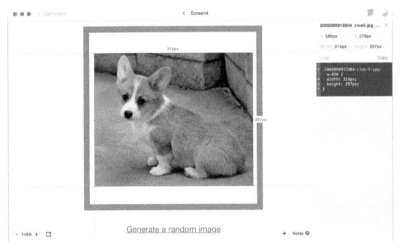

FIGURE 2-11
Redlines give specific dimensions and explain interactions for an interface

One way of providing details of a digital interface is to use supplementary software to create the redlines and style guides for you. One example is Zeplin, a tool that imports Sketch files and automatically adds redlines, extracts colors and font sizes, and displays them in an easy-to use reference guide (Figure 2-12). Designers and developers can both interact with the result to reference exactly which colors and spacing to create in the final, coded product.

Having a prototype for meetings and presentations highlights the idea better, and will help you to be taken seriously when you're presenting to future investors or collaborators. As a result, you'll have more faith in your idea, and feel more confident in your ability to communicate it appropriately. A prototype shows that you've put in thought and effort, and that you've personally invested in your idea. Your audience will feel more comfortable investing in you or your idea once they've seen this level of dedication.

FIGURE 2-12

Zeplin can save some work for you when you use it to communicate design details such as color and font styles to your developers

DEVELOPING A CULTURE OF PROTOTYPING

It's vital not only to prototype and have a personal mindset toward prototyping, but to create a culture of constant feedback and user testing on your team, in your company, and in your startup. Each person should feel comfortable seeking feedback from their peers to improve the work they are doing.

If this culture doesn't already exist in your company, you'll need to get it going. Start by displaying these behaviors and encouraging your peers to do the same. By trying out one of the ideas discussed here, you'll be on your way to incorporating feedback loops on all different levels of the company. When your coworkers begin to see how your work improves with constant user testing and prototyping, they'll reach out to you to help them with their work too. That way you can make prototyping a common term and an expected part of your team's process.

Try having a weekly feedback session where one or two people present their current work to get design, UX, or production feedback on it (Figure 2-13). Pull some of your coworkers aside and ask their opinion on a few different design options you're working on. These actions will help you break down your own biases and make sure you're not designing in a vacuum.

FIGURE 2-13
In-person critiques help improve your designs and build a culture of prototyping

Improve your meetings by requiring a prototype as a focus for the discussion, to keep everyone on track and make it easier to communicate about the work. Consider inviting coworkers (design, business, or development) or stakeholders to join you in observing a user testing session for extra backup. It's hard to deny that something's not working if you're confronted with an actual user struggling to use the current version.

If these ideas don't start building a culture of prototyping, try something different! Your process is a prototype, exactly like your work is.

To Test and Improve

Testing and improving products most likely will be the bulk of the prototypes you will make. At this point, you have an understanding of the problem you're tackling, and have lots of ideas of how to solve it for your users. You have sign-off from your stakeholders to move forward with the direction you presented. Instead of using your gut to choose the proper design and only testing the result once it's built and in users' hands, you can iteratively test small assumptions throughout your entire process and use that feedback to direct your design work (Figure 2-14).

FIGURE 2-14

Testing your ideas will help you choose the proper direction forward

It can be hard to make that first prototype. You might not have enough confidence in your idea to believe it's worth spending the time to prototype and test. But instead of spinning your wheels, and swirling around ideas in your head, start making. If you wait too long you will have too many assumptions to feasibly be able to test within one complicated prototype. Start prototyping as soon as you have any kind of idea in your head. Get it out and get other eyes on it. Talk about it. Test it. Improve it.

Once you're over the hurdle of the first prototype, you'll build up your own intuition about which assumptions are the most vital to test. Early in your process, you'll need to understand and test your user's mental model, or the way they perceive and understand the world and their thought process. Any piece of your product that assumes a user understands a specific word, categorization, use pattern, or navigation is ripe for testing (Figure 2-15). Make a few smaller tests that focus on each specific variable so that you can really understand what confuses the user, and fix it.

FIGURE 2-15
Navigation is very important to test for both terminology and mental model

If you're designing complex interactions that require technical understanding, you need to test it more often with your user because of your biased understanding of the product. At some point in your process, you will be so well informed about your technology and product that you will be too close to have the same perception as your user. Make sure you're testing your interface or product with both first-time and return users. Something that you think is well explained may turn out to be confusing to someone who hasn't seen it before.

Finally, each of the prototypes you make will be specifically designed for a unique assumption. The assumptions can be based on usability, proving value, or business strategy. Some examples include:

- Users can find their way to a specific feature

- The information architecture of the page is intuitive

- The user understands the chosen terminology and UI text

- The product and its functions is valuable enough for the amount of time it takes to use it

- A user can complete the ideal, full function of the product using the current interface design

This means that prototypes are disposable and most likely are not suited to test other, different assumptions. A specific prototype you create to test the information architecture of an app may not provide the necessary interactions for the user to determine the value of the app overall.

It may be painful to throw out a prototype, but after you've tested it and gained insights, the prototype has served its purpose and you must drive forward. The phrase "kill your darlings" doesn't only cover design elements that your users don't need; it refers to the artifacts that you create along the way. Prototypes are process artifacts, and once they've completed their job, it's time to move on.

Testing your ideas through prototypes will help you make better products, and will give you an informed direction forward. Instead of guessing what a user wants, you'll find value by interacting with them and gaining useful insights into their actual needs. And your team will benefit greatly from the user feedback you'll receive.

To Advocate

You can leverage prototypes and the insights you gain from testing them to advocate for the user experience and to support changes in direction or focus. When working with a larger team that includes product managers, business stakeholders, and a large development team, it's necessary to demonstrate the value and reasoning behind design decisions rather than simply showing them the visual results (Figure 2-16).

As a designer, you are the champion for the users, and it's your job to create the best, most intuitive design that will benefit them and solve their problems. The best way to do that is to have strong user testing results as evidence rather than relying on "the power of design" to get your ideas realized. You need to develop an ego-less designer approach. Bring humility to your work. Design is one part of a large ecosystem of product development. We provide value to the entire ecosystem, but not if we push our user agenda without taking other points of view into account. Try to have empathy with your team, as much as you build with your users, and provide value instead of roadblocks.

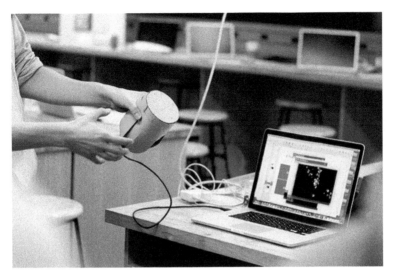

FIGURE 2-16
Use prototypes to demonstrate your idea and explain your design decisions

You should include your wider team in making and testing prototypes to build trust and to more quickly move development along (Figure 2-17). Try presenting your prototypes in team meetings and asking for feedback on them before user testing. Or work with the rest of the team to prioritize the assumptions that you'll be testing. Instead of pushing back on business or engineering input, listen and incorporate their suggestions into your prototypes in order to prove or disprove their assumptions too. By building bridges and including your whole development team in prototyping, your designs are more likely to gain acceptance and be implemented as designed.

For example, a business partner was concerned about "the fold" in a web-based product my team was creating. Much of the content for this product was a short scroll down the page, but not visible when you first land on the website. Although there is ample literature that debunks the myth of "the fold" in web pages, it took him sitting in on a user test and seeing users immediately scroll when they landed on the page before he trusted that the content would be seen. To make that happen, we invited him to observe some of the user testing, and we recorded the other tests so that he could experience for himself that there's no issue with a fold.

FIGURE 2-17
Include your stakeholders and coworkers when building and testing prototypes

You should try to incorporate your stakeholders' language of success and sales by using proper business terminology within your presentations and when you deliver results of user testing. At the end of the day, the better your user's experience is, the more marketable and useful your product will be and the more likely to be purchased or used by that user. The best way to improve the experience is to advocate for improvements to the interface or product based on the user testing insights. Keep this in mind as you share your work with stakeholders, and as you build the relationship between yourself and those who depend on your design work to improve their products.

Summary

Prototyping is beneficial for many reasons. The main four reasons are:

To understand
> Specifically, the user or problem that you're solving, and that the solution you're pursuing is the correct one for the user

To communicate
> Design directions to stakeholders, teammates, or clients; to get feedback on designs; and to specify final design details and interactions to developers, engineers, or manufacturers

To test

So that you can improve your ideas based on user feedback and validate or invalidate your assumptions

To advocate

For a specific direction or pivot, you'll need to convince your business stakeholders that it's the right decision based on user research results

One prototype might be used for multiple reasons—for example, to test then to communicate what happened in the test—but it's best to know the main reason for the prototype so you can build it appropriately and guide expectations. These four reasons for prototyping broaden the scope of when and how to use prototyping in your product development. You'll learn more about the process of prototyping for each of these reasons in Chapter 4.

To help stay focused in your development and to produce a product that solves a real problem, it's best to take a user-centered design approach. By keeping your ideal user in mind and their problem you're trying to solve as your focus, you can shape your product and test it with feedback from real people.

Finally, by incorporating prototypes into all parts of your design process, you can build a culture of prototyping at your workplace and among your peers. This environment will allow everyone to get constant feedback on their work, and improve the results of your work in a visible way.

[3]

Fidelity for Prototypes

CHOOSING A FIDELITY LEVEL is a critical part of creating a prototype. *Fidelity* means how closely the prototype looks and acts like the finished product. The proper fidelity level will focus the feedback you receive on the proper aspect of the design, so select your fidelity based on your goal for the prototype. Fidelity has varying levels (low, mid, and high, as well as mixed) and five dimensions (visual, breadth, depth, interactivity, and data model). It takes time and practice to learn which fidelity will enable you to get the feedback you need, but there are a few best practices for choosing.

The prototyping process usually benefits from starting with a low fidelity and slowly increasing the fidelity level until most of your assumptions are tested and either proved or fixed. You'll find that you make more prototypes earlier in the process, and fewer as your idea becomes more refined. It's necessary to be flexible and to decide which fidelity is right for each assumption you're testing along the way. If a prototype's fidelity level is too high, the user will subconsciously believe that the design is "finished" and will only give feedback on polishing areas instead of the broad concepts. If a prototype's fidelity is too low, the user might not understand the context and get lost in the generalities. There's also a balance between the time and effort it takes to make the prototype and the value you'll get from testing at that specific fidelity (Figure 3-1). By choosing the proper fidelity, or by creating a mixed fidelity, for your point in the process and the goal of the prototype, you'll save time and get the proper feedback you need to improve your ideas. I'll dig deeper into each aspect of fidelity next.

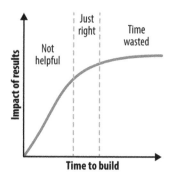

FIGURE 3-1

You must decide how much time and effort to put into a prototype based on its impact or value

Low Fidelity

Low-fidelity prototypes are best for testing your core concepts, getting over initial fears, thinking through many ideas, and catching potential problems before they get too big to fix. This type of prototype doesn't look like your final product at all; it's in a different medium, at a different size, and is usually not visually designed (although you should be thinking about visual design during this whole process).

It's the easiest and cheapest prototype to make, and doesn't require as much time or skill to complete. Some examples include paper prototypes, circuit building, storyboards, wireframes, mood boards, sketches, and component prototypes (Figure 3-2). The goal of a low-fidelity prototype is to test basic and big assumptions, including user flows; information architecture (labeling, navigation layout and basic organization); and user mental models. With this rough prototype, your user won't waste time giving feedback on the execution and appearance of the interface or device, and rather will focus on the overall use and flow of the product.

For example, when I'm working on the initial information architecture of a site (how a site is organized, what terminology to use for the specific user, and how to group labels in the most intuitive way), I first do a card-sorting activity (Figure 3-3). I give my user a set of cards that has all of my navigation pages and names on them and ask them to organize the cards in a way that makes sense for her or him. This activity allows me to understand my user's mental model because each individual will organize differently, and my navigation needs to work for all of these different mental models. It takes very little time, material, and effort to make a card-sorting activity, and I don't need an interface to test. I can learn a lot about my users, though, and improve the layout and navigation of my product to better suit them.

FIGURE 3-2
Low-fidelity prototypes take all sorts of forms and can test high level concepts (photo courtesy of Flickr user Dileck)

FIGURE 3-3
Card-sorting activities help you understand your user's mental model and indicate what to build for your next prototype

After card sorting, I immediately create a low-fidelity prototype of the proposed navigation or alternative navigation solutions with a little bit of the content on each page to give context. This prototype doesn't look like the final site—as shown in Figure 3-4, it's very basic and structural. But by asking people to find specific information, I can clearly see if they understand the navigation labels and how they're grouped, and how quickly they get to their goal. This testing informs the overall architecture of the site, and as I've learned firsthand, the architecture is difficult to change later in the process. By taking a small amount of time at the beginning of the process to test organizational assumptions, you can save time, pain, and hassle once the product nears completion.

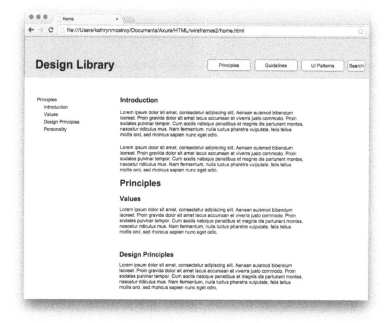

FIGURE 3-4

A low-fidelity IA prototype allows the user to interact with the navigation for better testing

Another example for low-fidelity is a breadboard-based circuit (Figure 3-5). You can try out your idea using a few specific components, and start by getting each component working on its own. Experimenting with low-fidelity circuits will help you decide which versions of the components you'd like to move forward with for higher-fidelity testing. Early in my process, I'll order a couple different types of microcontrollers, buttons and knobs, and LEDs to play with. The wider the variety of options I try out at a low fidelity, the more robust my final solution and next-round prototype will be. By testing these components separately, I also get a better feel for how they will come together in a circuit, and I can begin drawing out how the components will interact.

FIGURE 3-5
You can build low-fidelity circuits with a breadboard

Mid-Fidelity

Mid-fidelity prototypes start to look like your final product in at least one dimension (more on that momentarily). They are a good balance between cost (time or otherwise) and value. Mid-fidelity prototypes start to incorporate visual design, interactions, functionality, and the final medium (on the body, onscreen, in-browser, or physically designed). Some examples include clickable prototypes, style tiles, Axure prototypes, coded prototypes, and a variety of electronic prototypes (Figures 3-6 through 3-8).

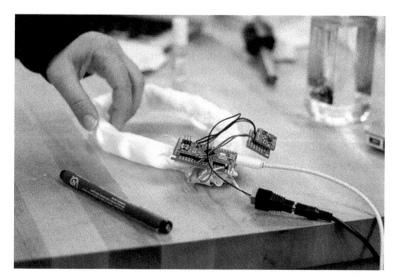

FIGURE 3-6

A mid-fidelity electronic prototype includes more interactive components

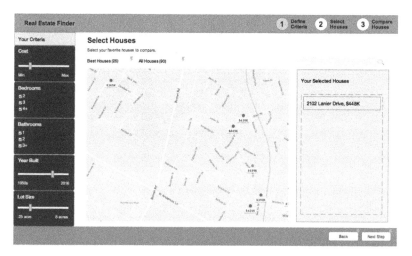

FIGURE 3-7

Mid-fidelity digital prototypes are more complex than their low-fidelity versions

Style Guide

Header/Footer bg   Subnav

f3f3f3   e6e7e8

Score card   Bars and radio buttons

cfd2d3   bbbdbf

Score colors

00b040   f9f402   da2809

"Thermometer" graphic colors

b9e7c9   f5d5bb   14bac0

Buttons and links

315d50

Footer graphics

66cac6   2e2e2e   f3f3f3

48 px **Page heading**

36 px **Let's get started!**

31 px **Section title**

24 px Subtitle

21 px Text

18 px Or paste an image URL

Score

Caption

Link

16 px

Body copy

Case Studies

Case Studies

315d50   d74106   6d6e71   828180

121212   2e2e2e

FIGURE 3-8

You can create style tiles to communicate the future visual design

Mid-fidelity prototypes should have a more refined assumption to test. One example is that a user can navigate through the whole user flow of a specific task. For a smart object, it might be that the user can understand the output lights and what they indicate (Figure 3-9). These prototypes take longer to make than low-fidelity ones, but you can begin testing more detailed parts of the interactions. The users will have more context in the prototype itself, which will give you more sound results in testing.

FIGURE 3-9

This mid-fidelity electronic prototype allows the user to control inputs and understand outputs better (photo courtesy of Flickr user svofski)

Mid-fidelity prototypes are useful for communication with stakeholders who might not have the ability to properly "read" low-fidelity work. You're showing a more refined view of the concept with better context. It's a good balance of the amount of time to make and more detail as to what you're building. With this fidelity level, the stakeholder doesn't have to imagine how the product will look in real life (either in a browser or as a physical object) and they can feel confident in the direction the design work is moving.

For example, when developing a wearable pacing arm band called Tempo, I made multiple mid-fidelity prototypes to test different aspects of the interactions and to communicate with my business stakeholder. The band uses a vibration motor to pulse a steady pattern onto the user's arm for meditation, pacing a run, and even as a silent metronome. One prototype allowed the user to change and set the pace of the pattern, but was a little too big to wear on a regular basis due to the low-fidelity components (Figure 3-10). So I made a separate, smaller prototype with a hardcoded pattern that the users could wear in their daily lives to give more in-depth feedback on its integration into their activities (Figure 3-11).

FIGURE 3-10
A fully functional, mid-fidelity prototype of my product idea

The former prototype helped me develop the smartphone app that allows the user to set and save patterns; the latter allowed me to improve the form and comfort of the actual, final wearable. Additionally, I used the second prototype to communicate the final size and scope of the product to my business stakeholder for their approval.

FIGURE 3-11
A non-customizable version of the arm band

Another example of mid-fidelity prototypes are clickable versions of your wireframes (Figure 3-12). You can use a program like PoP InVision, Proto.io, Flinto, or UXPin to quickly build simple prototypes to test your assumptions. Once you've made the mid-fidelity prototype, you can have the user interact with it on a specific device. You can have your smartphone app displayed on a smartphone template or have your user access it on the actual device to get feedback on the design in context.

FIGURE 3-12
You can make clickable versions of your wireframes with a variety of programs

High Fidelity

High-fidelity prototypes are the real deal. They are visually designed and are in the final medium of either physical materials or code in a browser. These prototypes have real content and most paths available to click or interact with. Some examples include a highly polished electronic smart object, a coded app, or a fully designed digital experience (Figure 3-13). At this point, most of your assumptions should have been tested in earlier prototypes. It's best to use this prototype to test small details like overall user reactions to the experience, animations or motion, legibility of the font sizes, long-term wearability, or size of the final buttons. High-fidelity prototypes cost more to make in time, skill level, and the software or coding needed to complete them.

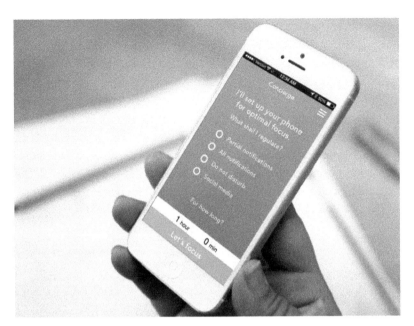

FIGURE 3-13
High-fidelity prototypes look like the real experience

At this point in the process, it's best to work with the team that will be involved with making your product: either developers, industrial designers, manufacturers, or electrical engineers. By collaborating with these teams to build prototypes, you are more likely to design something that's feasible to make, and able to be manufactured. If you're unable to work directly with these teams, but still need to test at a high fidelity, consult professionals for feasibility feedback. Then you can make complex digital prototypes with specific software like Sketch for visuals and Axure for interactions or physical prototypes using commercially available components. You can make high-fidelity physical prototypes by CNC milling, casting, sewing soft goods, or having circuit boards printed for you.

Here are some examples of aspects of a product that work well for testing in high fidelity, which I'll cover in more detail in Chapters 5 and 6:

- Testing animations
- Delightful elements, icons, and Easter eggs
- Specific user flow
- Entire use of the product

For example, toward the end of a software development release, engineering and design teams work together to build high-fidelity coded prototypes in the final product form so that after testing, if the results are positive, they can quickly ship the prototype into production (Figure 3-14). It's a bit risky because testing might still disprove some assumptions about the product, and the cost of building at high fidelity is high. But it gives one last layer of testing before releasing a product. Each release of a product is an opportunity to improve it, so even after shipping a final product, most Agile teams will continue to improve on the product based on user feedback and backlog of improvements.

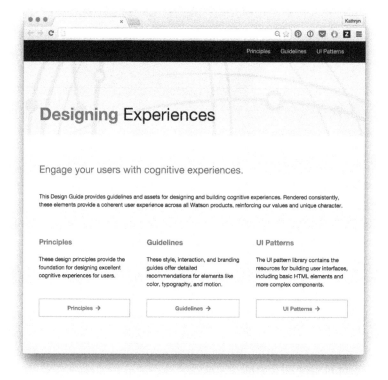

FIGURE 3-14

A production-level coded prototype might be able to be shipped if testing goes well

If you're having trouble choosing a fidelity level, use Table 3-1 as a cheat sheet.

TABLE 3-1. Pros and cons of each type of fidelity

	LOW FIDELITY	MID-FIDELITY	HIGH FIDELITY
Pros	Fast, low-skill, cheap, made with materials available around you	More interactive, easier to test, good balance of time and quality	Complete design, including visuals, content, and interactions; can test very detailed interactions
Cons	Limited interactions, harder to test details and full flows, little context for users	More time-intensive, but not fully functional	Very time-intensive, requires skills with software or coding, hard to test large concepts
Use	Exploring and testing high-level concepts like user flows and information architecture; best for making lots of different versions and testing them against each other	User testing specific interactions and guided flows; also better for stakeholder presentations, as these prototypes have more context	User testing very specific interactions and details, final testing of user flows, and presenting final design work to stakeholders

The Five Dimensions of Fidelity

In addition to pure low-, mid-, and high-fidelity prototypes, you can make a mixed-fidelity prototype by prioritizing the five dimensions of fidelity: visual refinement, breadth of functionality, depth of functionality, interactivity, and data model.[1] Depending on your goal for the prototype, you will likely have different fidelity levels for each dimension. By creating a custom mixed-fidelity approach, you'll be able to focus the feedback you receive on the specific part of the design. These five dimensions give you a fine-tooth approach to determining what to include in your prototype and how to mix a custom fidelity for your goal.

When I'm working on a prototype, I run my goal or assumption through these five dimensions to help me decide where to put my main making effort. Prioritizing which dimension is important for a specific prototype will help you focus and save you time and effort.

---

1 Michael Mccurdy et al., "Breaking the Fidelity Barrier," *Proceedings of the SIGCHI Conference on Human Factors in Computing Systems - CHI '06*, 2006. *doi:10.1145/1124772.1124959.*

VISUAL REFINEMENT

The visual refinement is what's typically thought of as fidelity, because it is the easiest way to make a prototype look like a finished product. Visual refinement is the amount of pixel-perfect design or material polish you've put into your interface or physical object.

Depending on your goal (e.g., understanding or testing), you might choose to have a lower fidelity in visual design to indicate the ideas are not solidified and are in process. Using lower-fidelity visuals, such as a boxy wireframe with sketchy lines or breadboards, will focus user feedback on the larger concepts of the user flow, instead of getting reactions to the colors, material choices, and intricate details (Figure 3-15).

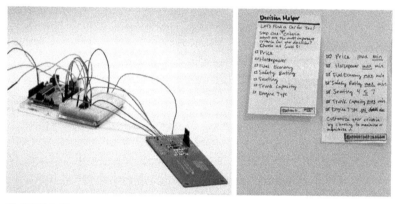

FIGURE 3-15
You may choose to use a low-fidelity prototype to get high-level feedback

Toward the end of your process, you'll want to test a higher-fidelity visual design to ensure the accessibility, touch and feel, and visual details are supporting the user (Figure 3-16). This prototype will be the opportunity to check contrast ratios, material interactions, aesthetic reactions, and legibility. You'll want users to experience the app or object in the natural environment and context that they will use it in.

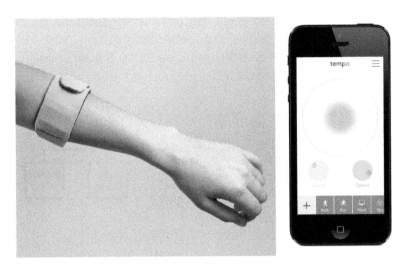

FIGURE 3-16
High-fidelity visuals allow you to test the touch and feel and accessibility of your designs

BREADTH

The breadth of the prototype indicates how much of the broad function-ality is represented in the prototype. You will not need the full breadth of the experience for every prototype you make. If you're smart about choosing the breadth fidelity, you'll save time and be able to move faster.

For example, if I'm creating a new music app or audio device where a listener can choose an album or song to play, can make playlists, and can purchase music, a higher-fidelity breadth would include all of these options as clickable in the interface or physical model (Figure 3-17). I can test how the user would use these different features together.

FIGURE 3-17
A high-fidelity breadth will allow the user to interact with all of the clickable features of an app

A lower fidelity of breadth might only focus on a single function, to make it easier to design and test that specific feature (Figure 3-18). The broader a prototype is, the better you can test the full set of tasks a user will interact with and the better you can test the full app or smart object's navigation.

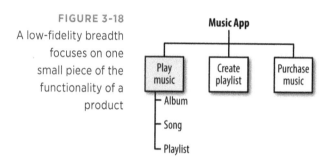

FIGURE 3-18

A low-fidelity breadth focuses on one small piece of the functionality of a product

When you map out the user flow of the product or site map of the app, you can decide how broad to make your prototype. You'll want to make a breadth that fits the assumption you're testing. You can indicate breadth by how many clickable elements, or interactive functions there are in the interface you present to the user.

DEPTH

The depth of the prototype indicates how detailed an individual feature of the prototype is built out to be. You can have one or multiple deep parts of the prototype, depending on the tasks you create for testing. Later in your process, your team (or multiple teams) might make many of the features deep so that the user can try different features of the product in one test.

For the same music app example, I might focus my user test on the playlist feature by building out the whole user flow for creating a playlist, and not creating the flow for purchasing music or playing songs or albums. Or I might create the buttons for scrolling through music options for the device (Figure 3-19).

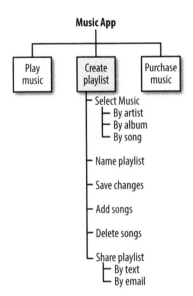

FIGURE 3-19

A high-fidelity depth contains all aspects of a specific function of the product

A higher fidelity in the depth of the features lets you test individual tasks the user will do within your product. A lower fidelity of depth is beneficial to test shallow navigation assumptions (Figure 3-20). The user does not need to interact deeply with a feature; they need to find how to get to it.

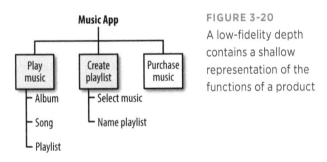

FIGURE 3-20

A low-fidelity depth contains a shallow representation of the functions of a product

You can make your prototyping time more effective if you balance the breadth and depth of your prototype based on your actual assumption's need (Figure 3-21). You might not need deep prototypes for your testing goal, but later in your process you might need a broad and deep prototype to test the entire environment.

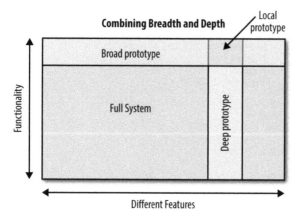

FIGURE 3-21

You can combine breadth and depth to create very effective and targeted prototypes (based on the concept by Neilsen)

INTERACTIVITY

The interactivity of the prototype indicates how the interactive parts of the app or product are displayed to the user. Some aspects include "call to action" buttons, physical buttons, how the page loads, LED reactions to button press, how interface elements animate, how the product reacts to user input, and the types of physical, visible, and audio outputs of electronics.

For our music app example, a low-fidelity interaction would be a paper prototype or mid-fidelity prototype that allows the user to "click" to different pages, but doesn't realistically show how the interface would move between those pages (Figure 3-22).

As I create a higher-fidelity interaction, I have the menu slide out from the side, and the names of the albums and artists slide into the list with a bit of a bounce.

Interactions provide crucial context through cues and choreography of parts for the user, so make sure you're testing this throughout your process. They can even set the voice and tone of the entire experience based on the reactions to the user (Figure 3-23). It's hard to test interactions at a low fidelity like paper prototypes or breadboard circuits. You'll need to use prototyping software or more in-depth microcontroller coding to help create animations and automated reactions to user input. There are some ways to fake these interactions, and I'll go into more detail on that in Chapters 5 and 6.

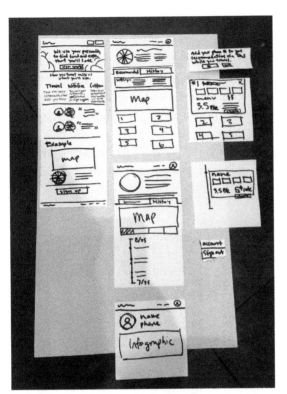

FIGURE 3-22
Low-fidelity
interactivity requires
manual movement and
does not include any
motion or transitions

FIGURE 3-23

High-fidelity interactivity includes clickable elements for inputs, animations and transitions, and outputs (photo courtesy of Flickr user Intel Free Press)

DATA MODEL

The data model encompasses the content that a user interacts with in the interface and the data utilized in both the frontend and backend of a product. Lower-fidelity content, such as lorem ipsum (dummy text), doesn't provide much context to the user, and might lead the user and the visual design astray by not providing a proper understanding of the content that will be on the page (Figure 3-24). It's important to have real data behind physical products too, so that you can assess specific backend structures andinformation processing, and find helpful code to help you move faster.

FIGURE 3-24

Low-fidelity data models might cause you to make mistakes in your design

If you don't have real data for your product, request it or create your own basic content that's similar to what your final content will be, or partner with developers to get the correct code and backend structures. This will allow you to test the tone and delivery of your messaging, or the voice of your smart object or wearable. You'll be able to update it when the real content is available, and your testing may inform how that content is written. Products should be designed around the real, final content, but sometimes you'll need to design quick, low-fidelity prototypes before the final content is ready.

When you use mid- to high-fidelity data, you'll improve your usability testing because the user will be able to reference real content (Figure 3-25). Your visual design will be able to take into account the proper scale and variety of outputs you'll need to display or store. For example, I could use fake song and artist titles in my music app prototype, but if I design with real data, I can make sure to take account of very long and very short names and descriptions within the interface design to ensure proper usage.

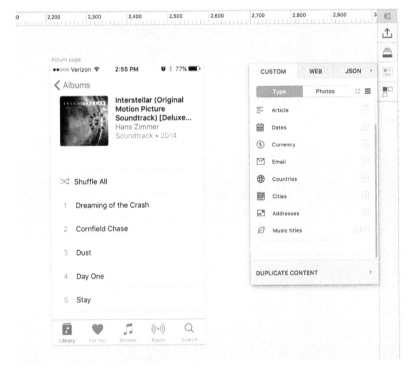

FIGURE 3-25
By using real song titles, you'll ensure you're leaving enough space for the extremes

Summary

Fidelity levels are a vital part of prototyping, and greatly affect the outcome of testing. You must choose the proper fidelity level depending on your goals and what part of the development process you are in.

- Low-fidelity prototypes are fast and cheap to make, and are good for testing high-level concepts.

- Mid-fidelity prototypes are a good compromise between time and quality, allowing you to test more specific questions, cast a vision, and communicate with stakeholders better.

- High-fidelity prototypes take the most investment in time and skills, and allow you to test fine-tooth details. They're great for selling a concept to a client, and finalizing work. They're also good for communicating final design decisions to developers so that they can implement the work.

You can use the five dimensions of prototypes to create custom mixed-fidelity prototypes using visual refinement, breadth, depth, interactivity, and data models. One prototype can have different fidelities for each of these dimensions in order to fulfill a specific goal. It takes time to develop the skills to know which fidelity to use for each situation, but these examples have given you a good foundation to start applying to your work.

[4]

The Process of Prototyping

YOUR PROTOTYPING PROCESS WILL take a slightly different path depending on the purpose for each prototype, and the process can vary depending on your goals, audience, and assumptions (Figure 4-1).

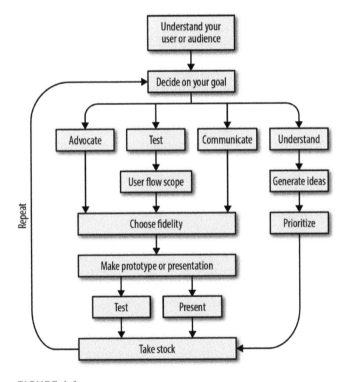

FIGURE 4-1

The process of prototyping depends on your goals, audience, and assumptions

To choose the proper process to follow, use these guidelines.

- Are you trying out prototyping, or don't know what to do first? Try making a "minimum viable prototype."

- Is your purpose to generate lots of different solutions for a problem? Then your process will be focused on exploration.

- Will you use the prototype to communicate or advocate for a certain direction? Then you need to concentrate on your specific audience.

- Do you have a question or assumption to test? Your process will be focused on that assumption.

Establishing the goal and focus of your process will ground your prototype, and limit the scope so that it doesn't get too difficult to make.

Minimum Viable Prototype

If you don't know where to start, you have limited time, or you want to try out prototyping before applying it to your work, use this process as a guide. A minimum viable prototype is the least amount of effort and a generalized approach to building a prototype. It will be the first step to becoming more comfortable with incorporating prototyping into your day-to-day work.

STEP 1: ESTABLISH WHO YOUR USERS ARE AND IDENTIFY THEIR PROBLEM

To start, review the material in Chapter 2 about understanding your users and their problem. Once you have a good idea of the pain point or problem you're solving for your users, think of a few different ways to solve that problem. If you want more guidance on exploration, skip to the section "Exploration-Centric."

For example, I have a user who is a female, young professional, and owns a dog, but must travel a lot for work. She has a dogsitter, but wants regular check-ins to see her dog and to connect with it. Currently, there are a few expensive smart objects that allow her to view or interact with her pet, but she has to manually log in, turn on the camera, and hope her dog is in view. From these pain points—expensive tech, manual login, not guaranteed to see the dog—I see an opportunity area to create a new product for this user.

I can solve this problem a few different ways, but after exploring and testing three different ideas, I've decided to make a lower-resolution camera connected to a motion sensor that's mounted at dog-height near the dog's food and water. The camera will automatically take pictures of the dog when it walks by, and texts these pictures to the user, not requiring her to have an app or manually log in. But if users want more control, they can download an accompanying smartphone app that allows them to angle the camera, and talk to their dog. Now I'm ready for the next step.

STEP 2: WRITE OUT A USER FLOW THAT SOLVES THEIR PROBLEM

Now that you have a user, a problem, and a direction to solve it, you're ready to create the user flow that supports that direction. A user flow is the journey the user takes to complete their goal. You can write it out in sentences, make a diagram, or draw it as a storyboard. Figure 4-2 shows how that looks for a shopping checkout experience.

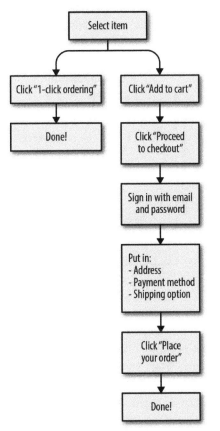

FIGURE 4-2

This user flow demonstrates how one checks out on Amazon

Your user flow will help you determine the scope of the prototype that you need to create, or the extent of the subject matter that a prototype covers. If your main pain point is the signup process of an app, you don't need to include the entire functional usage of your app in the prototype. Start by prototyping, testing, and improving the signup process. By prioritizing and scoping your work properly, you'll save time and be able to focus on very tangible results faster. You'll be able to limit the variables that affect the user's experience. You can isolate smaller areas to test, then incorporate them all together to test the full product experience. This scoping exercise is especially helpful with electronics, to ensure that the different components are functioning before combining them together.

If you don't have an obvious scope within your user flow, look for assumptions that are not backed by research (which might be everything), and prioritize which assumption is the most crucial to test first (Figure 4-3). One way to determine priority is to ask yourself "if this assumption is false, will it block the product from being useful or selling?" You'll want to start with the one that would completely derail your product if it's wrong.

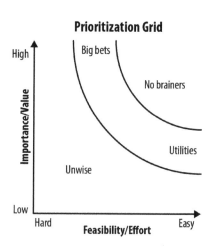

FIGURE 4-3

You can prioritize your assumptions based on the value it will have versus the time or effort it would take to test it

For example, the UI text you choose for your navigation might not match your user's mental model. If you choose witty text instead of direct terminology, your user might not understand how to find specific functions of your product (Figure 4-4). So the best prototype to start with would be one to test your navigation and call-to-action text to make sure your user understands what it means.

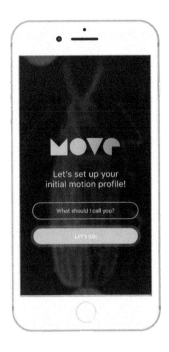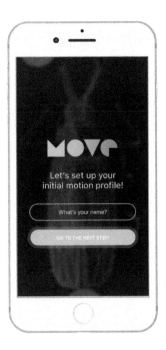

FIGURE 4-4

Testing your call-to-action text is a high priority

Another example is choosing the icon types for a smart object interface (Figure 4-5).

FIGURE 4-5

Icons should be tested in order to make sure your user understands what they represent

For our example, I've made a user flow and found a few interesting assumptions that will need to be tested (Figure 4-6).

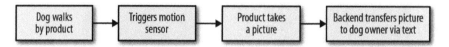

FIGURE 4-6

The user flow for the motion-triggered dog watcher indicates a few different major assumptions

One assumption is that the dog will be active enough to trigger a motion sensor. Another is that the images the camera takes will be good enough to make it worth texting to the owner. The former is a huge deal breaker; if the dog doesn't trigger the camera, then there's no product. The latter is something that can be fine-tuned after the launch. So I now know that I need to make a prototype to test my motion sensors with real dogs to see how much motion is needed to trigger the sensor.

STEP 3: MAKE THE PROTOTYPE TO ADDRESS THE USER FLOW

Take the user flow that you've written or diagramed and draw wireframes or combine the necessary electrical components that you need to create the prototype that you require. At this point, you'll need to choose what fidelity level would be best. Read Chapter 3 for details on how to choose a fidelity level.

Overall, you'll want to use a low-fidelity prototype early in your process, and gradually increase the fidelity level as your idea becomes more refined. You'll need to choose your medium for this prototype such as a paper prototype, coded or interactive prototype, breadboard-based prototype, or unit-test prototypes (more about each one of these in Chapters 5 and 6).

Draw out the screens, or write code for the components, for each step that you decided is crucial to test. Ensure that your prototype is addressing the assumption you're trying to improve. Figure 4-7 shows an example of a quick paper prototype for testing the navigation of a celebrity news app.

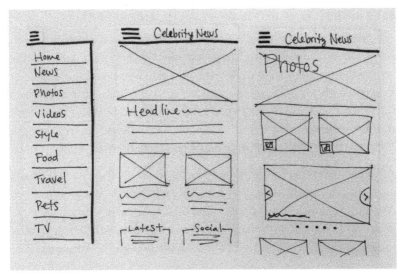

FIGURE 4-7

Once you decide the assumption you're testing, you can build a specific prototype to address it

For the motion sensor prototype for our new dog product, I've put together a quick breadboard prototype with a motion sensor, an Arduino microcontroller, and an LED light (Figure 4-8). With these two components and a little bit of code, I can see exactly how much motion it takes to set off the sensor. The code I'm using will turn on the LED light whenever it sees motion, and turn it off after the motion stops. Now I'm ready to set up and test the prototype.

FIGURE 4-8

A low-fidelity prototype will help me understand how much motion the dog needs to make to register with my sensor

STEP 4: TEST, TAKE STOCK OF RESULTS, AND REPEAT

Now you're ready to test the prototype! Write up your research plan (see Chapter 7 for details), find a few users to test with, and observe what went well and what didn't. It's best to have an additional person help you with your user test so you can ask questions and they can take notes. Keep in mind that it's a good thing if the user gets lost or doesn't complete the task properly. That means you've found an area you can improve, and that the prototype was a good use of time.

After testing with a few different people (shoot for four to eight, based on the advice outlined in Erika Hall's *Just Enough Research* [A Book Apart]), take stock of your notes. Did a pattern emerge from the feedback? Was your assumption validated or invalidated? Did any other insights pop up randomly that you didn't previously consider? Take these insights back to your original user and problem, and think through how you can improve the experience. Go back through this process and make another prototype with a newly prioritized list of assumptions based on your user testing.

Finally, for our new dog product, I was able to test with a few different breeds and sizes of dogs to check for the proper motion sensor calibration (Figure 4-9).

FIGURE 4-9
I tested the prototype with a few different dogs and environments

Based on the tests, the sensor should not necessarily be near the food bowl, but positioned in the common room in which the dog spends the most time. That way, when the dog jumps up on the couch or curls up on his dog bed, the camera will capture the dog at its best. The next round of prototyping will focus on the owner's interactions with the device, and designing a prototype of the smartphone app.

Exploration-Centric

The exploration-centric process spends more time on generative ideation and less time on creating prototyping artifacts. However, it's helpful to think through ideas in an interactive way, instead of merely through sketches or wireframes. Your goal for exploring is to find the right problem to solve, to make an educated decision on the way or ways to solve the problem, and to set yourself up so you can communicate and test many variations on that solution with later prototypes. This process is loose and open because it's at the beginning of a project and you haven't made many decisions yet. Start with understanding your user and their problem as stated in the opening paragraphs of this chapter.

STEP 1: GENERATE LOTS OF WAYS TO SOLVE THE USER'S PROBLEM

Using Post-its and Sharpies (or any other drawing method) loosely draw or write out one solution idea per Post-it and immediately put it up on a wall (Figure 4-10). Some ideas will seem obvious and others will seem downright crazy. By getting all the obvious solutions out in the open, you can go beyond low-hanging fruit and think of innovative ways to solve the problem. Make sure you're not editing yourself; put up ideas that seem off the wall. You will find insightful bits from those crazy ideas that will inform and improve a more solid approach.

This ideation exercise can be done solo or with your whole team. With a group of people, you can riff off one another's ideas as they're placed on the wall. Use sketches as a jumping-off point for discussions, and create an atmosphere of positive building. When I start hearing a lot of "nos" and "we can't," I have the group employ a tactic from improv comedy called "Yes, and..."—instead of negating a teammate's idea, you find a way to say "yes, and" to build on it. This tactic allows everyone to feel more comfortable sharing and creating ideas, when they know that it won't immediately be shot down (Figure 4-11).

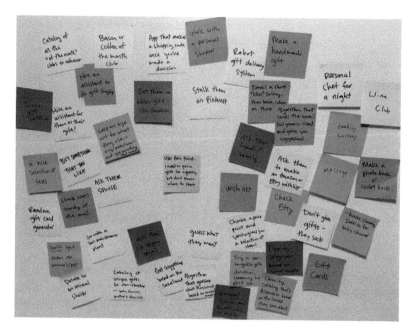

FIGURE 4-10

An ideation session brainstorm

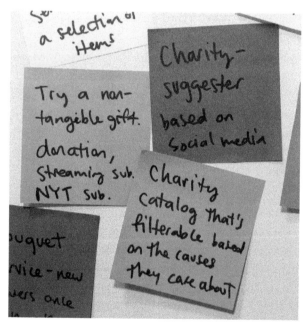

FIGURE 4-11

Two ideas that build off each other

Alternatively, you can perform this activity remotely by using the variety of different "sticky note" software options, including Mural, Post-it Plus, or Stormboard (Figure 4-12). Make sure your full team participates, including design, development, and business partners. Have everyone call in to a conference call and then moderate the session with quiet periods for adding ideas on Post-its, then discussion periods to answer questions and generate more ideas.

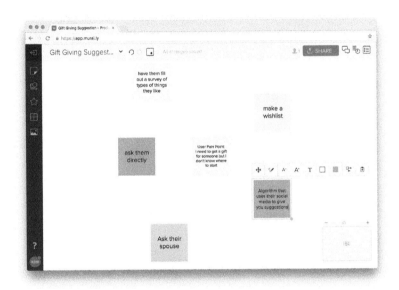

FIGURE 4-12
Online collaboration software is a good way to include remote teammates in ideation

STEP 2: GROUP SIMILAR IDEAS TOGETHER
TO CREATE OVERALL CATEGORIES

As your wall, or web page, begins to fill with ideas, and after the participants start slowing down with their ideas, begin grouping the ideas into similar topics or solutions, in a process called *affinity mapping* (Figure 4-13). These similar categories will show you the strongest directions forward, and give you a few specific ideas to begin prototyping. Try not to lose the unique ideas within these more generalized categories as you move forward. Instead, look for the common elements that make a strong solution, and build off of the individual ideas. As a team, you can vote with stickers or dots to prioritize which solutions would be most beneficial to the user. Or you can do research on the solution categories to help direct the team forward.

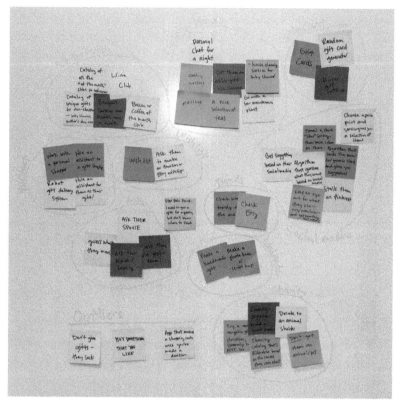

FIGURE 4-13
Group your Post-its into categories

During the ideation, keep track of assumptions as you hear them (Figure 4-14), and make sure to research those points by talking to users at a later time. You might hear "the user wants this feature" or "the user will use our product specifically this way." If someone makes a confident statement from the user's point of view, make sure to ask if it's backed by direct quotes or research insights or if it's based on gut instinct. Since you're early in your process, it's a great opportunity to learn more about the existing user problems and to find additional or alternative pain points. By determining what statements are assumed or valid, you'll gain more confidence that you're solving the right problem before you get too far into the development process. You'll have better alignment with your team up front, which will prevent later problems.

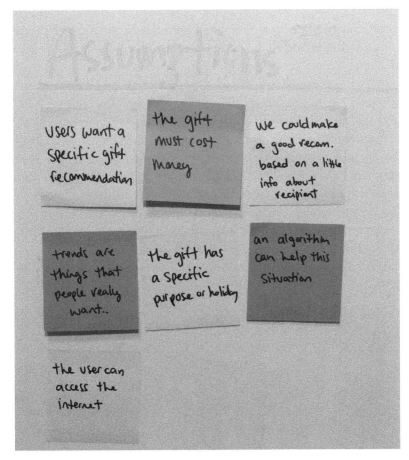

FIGURE 4-14
Keep track of your assumptions throughout your ideation session

For example, suppose you're working on a new social app for photographers, and your business stakeholder makes a statement about the user's point of view such as "the main use case for our user is to post images." It's delivered as a researched statement, so you don't test it as an assumption. But much later in the process, when you're neck deep in testing prototypes, you discover that the main use for your photographer user is to see and consume other people's images as inspiration. That's a major difference in use case and changes how you would design the user flow. By knowing up front that the use case is an assumption, you would have the opportunity to do additional research with users, before wasting time building prototypes, to confirm or deny that idea. That way, you can pivot early and save time and money.

Another way to think from your user's point of view is to do a bodystorming activity in addition to Post-it brainstorming. Bodystorming is performance-based ideation where your team role-plays specific users and situations to understand how that user currently deals with their problems and how they might interact and react to your new ideas (Figure 4-15). You can use bodystorming to act out interactions with physical objects or with digital software. Gather the necessary artifacts—such as Post-its, Sharpies, boxes, or paper—to set up a low-fidelity interaction (see Chapters 5 and 6 for more details). Use your team and act out the entire user flow, while recording it. Based on your reaction to how the interaction felt, make slight changes and try it again, improving and changing your situational prototype. This opportunity is great for trying crazy ideas, since it's such a low barrier to test it out. For more information or detailed directions on bodystorming, check out *Gamestorming* (O'Reilly).

FIGURE 4-15

Unsworn set up a faux train to test an idea in a physical space (photo courtesy of Flickr user Unsworn Industries)

For example, a new online shopping experience can be bodystormed by setting up an actual store and seeing how people interact with objects displayed in different ways on a shelf or how they check out. These insights can be translated into a shopping metaphor that the user interacts with online, but is familiar with because it's based on how they interact in real life.

STEP 3: DECIDE A DIRECTION FORWARD
BASED ON YOUR PRIORITIZATION

Look over your prioritized solution direction and determine which one or two ideas to take forward into actual prototyping (Figures 4-16 and 17). With each set of ideas, keep in mind and write down the assumptions that are built in and that need to be tested as part of prototyping. From this point, you can jump straight to the assumption-centric process to continue with prototyping the idea.

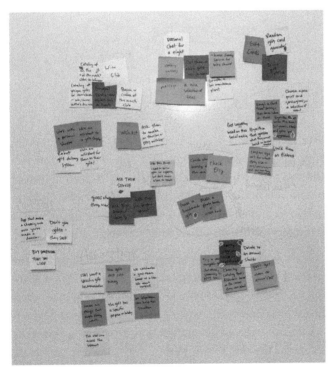

FIGURE 4-16

You can vote on the best ideas with dots

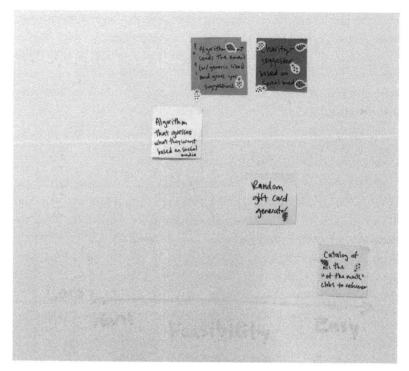

FIGURE 4-17
Or you can decide which direction to go based on a prioritization grid

During and after these exercises, make sure to revisit the initial problem you're solving for your user and decide if it's the proper and correct one to solve. Did you come across any alternative problems that impact the user more? Did you find a different direction to solve the problem that would be easier to implement and more impactful for the user? Are your solutions completely different than what you originally expected?

Discuss this process with your entire team, if they weren't part of the ideation, and present the findings to your stakeholders to help the team make a decision on how to move forward. Documentation is a necessary part of the exploration-centric process. You need to be able to reference this work if you need a different direction, after you've tested the highest-priority ideas. You don't want to reinvent the wheel, so ensure that your team can access and learn from the process work that you've done. My team keeps a cloud-based folder to hold our ideation artifacts (pictures of Post-it brainstorms, grouping, and prioritized solutions), and we host much of our research and design work in an internal GitHub Wiki for the development and business teams to access.

Audience-Centric

The process of prototyping for communication has a big emphasis on the audience and what you're trying to get across in your communication. This process can be used throughout product development to communicate at different points in time to different people. The goal is to make it clear what you're designing in order to gain approval, get feedback, or obtain alignment for decision-making or implementation. Any time that you communicate with someone, it is helpful to have a prototype to focus the conversation, and to provide a specific example to talk about.

STEP 1: DETERMINE YOUR AUDIENCE, YOUR GOAL, AND THE FIDELITY LEVEL

You will have many audiences and goals throughout the project. Start by thinking through who you will be speaking with and why you're speaking with them. Are you talking with fellow designers for feedback? Is this a stakeholder presentation to get approval? Are you selling a concept to a client? Are you explaining a final design to a developer?

It's vital to understand the audience's background and how much they already know about your product. Each of these audiences needs a specific context set for them to help them understand your ideas.

Designers
> Good to ask for feedback, support, critique, and ideation.

Stakeholders
> Good for getting approval of design direction, check-ins on progress, and affirming that the business needs are being met.

Clients
> Similar to stakeholders, they need check-ins to assure that you're on track with the work, and before then they need to be sold on the idea so that they will sign a contract with you.

Developers/engineers
> Good to ask for input on feasibility throughout the design process and to communicate final design decisions to, so that they can create the product.

Your goal can be getting buy-in for a design decision, getting feedback for a specific interaction area, or showing the functionality in an easier to understand way. You will have a much different prototype if your goal is to get feedback from fellow designers than if you're selling a client or stakeholder on the direction you've chosen. Make a decision on what you want to achieve with this communication. Choose one goal and one audience; otherwise your message will be muddied.

Based on the audience and goal, choose what type of language and visual style you need to use. For designers, you can be more casual in your approach. Set the context and clear expectations for what type of feedback you need; otherwise you might end up in a rabbit hole discussing kerning when you need help with navigation flows.

For stakeholders and clients, you'll need to talk in business terms, including the time to market, unique value propositions, and the value of the design tasks in real, measurable numbers (Figure 4-18). For developers, you'll need to discuss frameworks, code bases, performance budgets, and where to submit software issues.

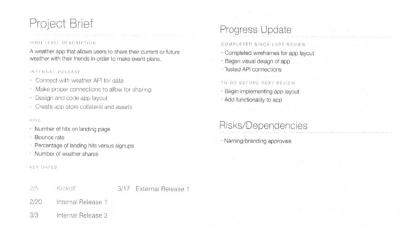

FIGURE 4-18

Use the correct terminology when communicating with business stakeholders

Finally, choose which fidelity you need:

Designers

> Can understand lower-fidelity work and give feedback on ideas and concepts, and can critique higher-fidelity work to help improve the fine details that make the experience better. Choose a fidelity level to direct the type of feedback you want from them.

Stakeholders

> Can understand low-fidelity work for concepts, user flows, and early alignment and mid- to high-fidelity mock-ups or prototypes of the solution and later work. Make sure to set expectations for the group as to how far into the process you are, what is still being worked on (such as visuals, interactions, or layout), and what you believe will change before the next presentation. Mid-fidelity prototypes are usually the best bet because it will indicate that the work is still in progress.

Clients

> Need to understand the concept in a realistic way through a mid- to high-fidelity prototype. Show how the idea will work with their existing brand and style guides. You might show a mid-fidelity prototype for them to interact with and a high-fidelity mock-up of the visuals for them to see how it might look in their lineup of other products. Continue to set expectations for them on what work you will deliver while showing them the prototype of where the work is going in the future.

Developers/engineers

> Can understand lower-fidelity work, but give the best feasibility feedback on mid- to high-fidelity prototypes when they can better understand the difficulty of implementation for coding or engineering. High-fidelity work is necessary to communicate final design decisions that need to be included in the development work.

For example, I'm designing a weather-based app and my audience is made up of business stakeholders and a team of engineers who will be implementing the design. I do a few rounds of ideation and design at a low fidelity. When I'm ready to present the idea to the full team, I decide that my goal is to get business sign off on the design direction and feasibility feedback from the engineers. I decide to build a mid-fidelity prototype for this audience and goal (Figure 4-19).

FIGURE 4-19

I chose to build a
mid-fidelity prototype
based on my user
flow to communicate
with my business
stakeholders and
engineers

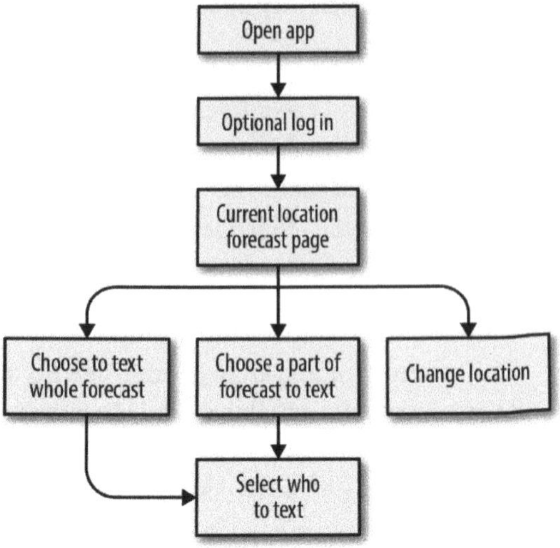

```
           ┌──────────────┐
           │   Open app   │
           └──────┬───────┘
                  ▼
           ┌──────────────┐
           │ Optional log in │
           └──────┬───────┘
                  ▼
           ┌──────────────┐
           │ Current location │
           │  forecast page  │
           └──────┬───────┘
```

| Choose to text whole forecast | Choose a part of forecast to text | Change location |

Select who to text

STEP 2: WHAT DO YOU NEED TO INCLUDE TO REACH YOUR GOAL?

The next decision you need to make is what to include in the prototype to communicate and achieve your goal. Do you need a certain level of functionality or will the basic clickable wireframing be enough information? Do you need to communicate specific, intricate details or overarching directions?

If you want feedback from designers, you might not need an entire user flow; rather, show the segment that provides context to the problem you need help with. You can get feedback on the user flow itself, or on the experience of the app or product.

For stakeholder or client sign-off, you'll need to represent most of the user flow and full experience of the product (Figure 4-20). That way, they have a better understanding of the design direction and why you've made certain decisions.

For development, you'll need to target the parts of a product that are assumed feasible, but haven't been confirmed. Motion and animations for digital products are a good example of work that you need to communicate to developers (Figure 4-21). Intended sensor inputs and outputs are an example for physical products. Make sure to include enough detail so your developers or engineers don't get surprised later down the line with additional requests and features.

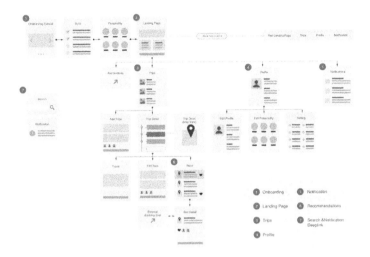

FIGURE 4-20

A higher-fidelity user flow (in the dimension of depth and breadth) is often a good choice for certain stakeholders (image courtesy of Sushi Sutasirisap)

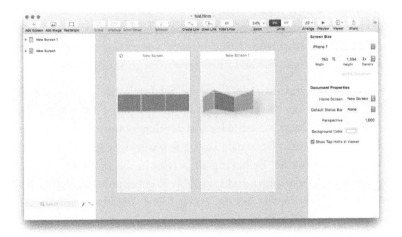

FIGURE 4-21

It's important to communicate motion and animations to your developers early on (image courtesy of Flinto.com)

For my weather app example, I'll need to include real content (such as temperatures, radar, and humidity), explanations of the interactions, and the full user flow. By creating a more complex prototype, I'll be able to have real discussions about the business implications of the design from my stakeholders and the feasibility of the development from my engineers.

STEP 3: PRESENT THE PROTOTYPE TO YOUR AUDIENCE

It's best to present the prototype through a story, using the user persona to walk through the portion of the user flow you decided to include. Give enough context at the beginning of your presentation so that your audience knows what the goal of the presentation is. If you need feedback with a specific interaction, call it out. If you need sign-off from the stakeholder before moving to user testing, specifically state that need. The more explicit you are in your request, and the better you set your audience's expectations, the more useful the presentation and reactions will be.

After you present, take clear notes on the feedback you receive. Not every comment will be useful, but go through each person's thoughts and look for the nuggets of wisdom that will help you move your project forward. If you obtain your goal (feedback, approval, a signed contract), acknowledge the success and move forward with your insights.

For the weather app example, I received feedback that it would take too much time to make the animations in the app based on our timeline. Because the business stakeholder and developers were in the presentation, we moved the release date back a few weeks to accommodate the development timeline. By having all parties in the same presentation, the team was able to align, and I was able to get approval from the business stakeholders for the design, and get feedback from the engineers about how the work will be implemented.

Assumption-Centric

An assumption-centered prototype is one that you test in order to improve your idea and product. It can be based on a hypothesis, question, or assumption. Sometimes that assumption will be broad: "the user is able to find their way through an app and accomplish the tasks within the app interface." Other times the assumption will be very specific: "the user can wear a new smart object all day without it annoying them."

This process can be quick or take a long time, depending on the fidelity level and the interactions that are required to test that assumption. You might be able to accomplish two rounds of iterative testing in a day, or it might take you an entire sprint cycle or more to build a prototype to test.

STEP 1: DETERMINE YOUR USER, THEIR PROBLEM, AND THE ASSUMPTION YOU NEED TO TEST

Similar to the other processes, start with your well-defined user and their problem. Then, based on your user flow or previous prototyping results, write out which assumption you're focusing on this round to keep yourself on task for creating the prototype (Figure 4-22). If you have too many assumptions, or if they don't relate, break up the process into multiple prototypes so you can focus on one aspect at a time.

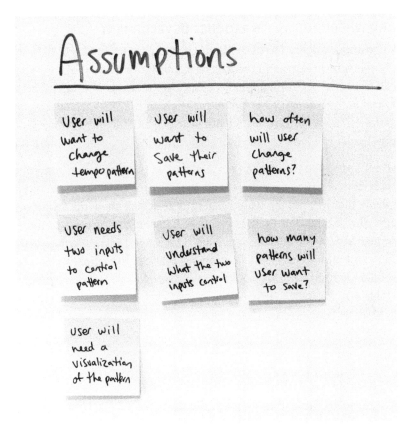

FIGURE 4-22

Review your assumptions and determine which ones you need to test

This is true for both digital products and physical products. If you're working with multiple types of electronic inputs and outputs, such as a pulse sensor and a touch screen output, you'll want to test these components separately to work out the code and how the individual parts should work together before combining them.

For example, I created many different levels of testing for Tempo, a wearable haptic pacing device that I referenced earlier. It pulses a slow, steady pattern onto the user's arm to help them be present in the moment or to be more productive at work. For one specific round of prototyping, I needed to test the assumption that the user would understand how to control and set the pacing pattern of the device. I'll walk through how I designed the prototype and tested it in each of the following steps.

STEP 2: PICK A FIDELITY LEVEL BASED ON YOUR ASSUMPTION AND WHERE YOU ARE IN PRODUCT DEVELOPMENT

Choosing a fidelity level can seem tricky at first, but it will help to ground your prototype in the part of the design process you're in. You can test at the beginning, middle, or near your release date, but it's best to test early, before it's too late to make changes. The specific type of assumption will inform the fidelity too, such as content-based, navigation-based, full-flow, or individual task-based.

Overall, if you're early in the process, and working on larger concepts such as navigation, user flows, and general functions, choose a lower fidelity that will put the focus on getting feedback about the terminology, flow layout, and basic interaction. Later in the process, as more content becomes available or your smart object gets more sophisticated, you can build higher-fidelity prototypes that put the emphasis on the details, such as user understanding, task completion, and visual design (Table 4-1).

TABLE 4-1. Your fidelity level will depend on the scope and type of
assumption you're testing

FIDELITY LEVEL	LOW	HIGH
Assumptions about...	• High-level concepts • Navigation • Terminology • User flows • General functionality • Who your user is	• Completing tasks • User understanding • High-fidelity navigation • Visual design details like iconography and typography • Written content

You can decide which fidelity dimensions you should emphasize. If
your assumption needs a full user flow, you'll need a higher-breadth
fidelity. However, if your assumption is based on one function within
the app, it will need depth into that task flow. The data model and content of your prototype can greatly affect the context for the user, so as
you choose a fidelity level, make sure to include real content for text,
images, and smart object outputs like lights, text responses, and tactile
responses.

For my Tempo example, I was early in the process, so I knew I needed
a low- to mid-fidelity prototype. The function of changing and making
new patterns would be part of a smartphone app, but at this part of the
process, I was not using a smartphone interface yet. So I decided to
make an analog version of the interaction with a few potentiometers
(dials) that are connected to a microcontroller and vibration motors as
outputs (Figure 4-23). That way, the user could change the two variables associated with the pattern (the assumption in question) without
needing to touch a smartphone.

FIGURE 4-23

Breadboard of the
mid-fidelity prototype
with potentiometers to
control the output

STEP 3: DECIDE THE TYPE OF TEST YOU SHOULD DO

Choose what type of testing you'll need to do based on the assumption you have and the fidelity level you're working with. The lower-fidelity, large-concept assumptions might utilize tests such as card sorts or basic click-throughs. If you have multiple ideas for a specific interaction point, you might want to conduct an A/B test, which would require multiple versions of the same prototype. If you're testing the functionality of the app or smart object, you'll want to use a task-based test to see if the user completes the task in the same manner that you assume they will.

The type of test and the prototype fidelity inform each other, in a chicken-and-egg kind of way. As you prototype more, you'll start to build a gut feel for how these two pieces work together.

Once you've decided which type of test you'll conduct, take a few minutes to create a research plan. I go into great detail about research in Chapter 7. A research plan starts with the assumption and goal of the test, then gives a profile of the type of user you'd like to test with a few establishing questions, and finally goes through the tasks and follow-up questions that you'll have the user do. By writing out this plan before you build your prototype, or during the building, you'll make sure you're building the right functionality and pages that you'll need to test the specific tasks.

For my smart wearable, I decided to create a research plan for a task-based test. I wrote out the goal and user profile, and created tasks for them to accomplish (Figure 4-24).

STEP 4: BUILD THE PROTOTYPE

With your fidelity level chosen, and your research plan written, you're ready to build the prototype you need to test your assumption. I go into great detail about how to build all different levels of prototypes for both smart objects and software in Chapters 5 and 6, respectively. Keep in mind what you're trying to accomplish, and make sure you don't allow your prototype scope to increase unknowingly. Only build what you need to in order to test your assumption.

Tempo Research Plan

Goals and assumptions
- Determine if a user can create a new tempo pattern
- Understand how the user would create, save, and use patterns
- Determine if the pattern needs two inputs or one

User profile
- Young professionals in the tech industry, mostly works on computers and gets distracted by social media and internet rabbit holes
- Variety of users who are physically active in different ways

Establishing questions
- Name
- Job description
- How often are you distracted during work hours or during the day?
- What are the main causes of this distraction?
- How do you currently deal with distractions?

Tasks
- You are at work and trying to focus on finishing a specific task. How would you create a pulse pattern that will help you stay focused?
- You are giving a presentation to a large group of people. What pattern would you use for this situation?
- Outside of work, you are using the Tempo band for other activities. What activity would you use it for, and create a pattern for that activity.
- Now that we're finished, what were your top two aspects and bottom two aspects of this experience?
- How do you see the Tempo fitting into your life and activities?

FIGURE 4-24

The research plan has goals and task questions for Tempo

Don't forget that you might not use this prototype again after this round of testing, especially if you iteratively change the design based on the insights. Don't get too attached to the specific prototype beyond the user test. Make sure you'll be comfortable throwing out the prototype once it's met its purpose, which is to give you insights from user testing.

For Tempo, I chose my microcontroller, an Arduino Micro, for its size and functionality. I used two vibration motors for the output, and two potentiometers for the input. I then soldered them all together and sewed the outputs into an arm band (Figure 4-25). The quality of the armband was not important to this test. Neither was the fact that there were wires running from the armband to the microcontroller. As long as the user could change the patterns with the two dials, the prototype would be a success.

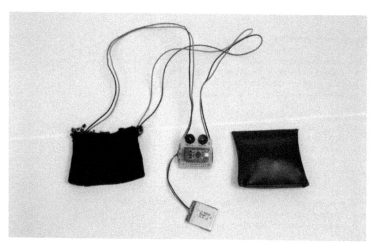

FIGURE 4-25
The final prototype for the mid-fidelity Tempo test

I could have easily spent more time making a more aesthetic or wireless model for this test, but it would have gotten the same results. Since I made a fast and dirty prototype, I was able to more quickly move on to my next assumption to test.

STEP 5: TEST YOUR PROTOTYPE

With your prototype in hand, on screen, or on a breadboard, you're ready to conduct your user testing. Gather the necessary people and tools you'll need to run your test. Overall, you'll want at least one other helper to take notes for you while you ask the user questions and pose tasks to them. With permission, you can record their interactions with a camera or screen recording, in order to revisit the interview and take your own notes or as support to show your stakeholder.

In the test, try not to give away too much. If the user wanders off the "happy path" (or the expected way of completing the task), take note but don't redirect them too quickly. You might get insightful information from what they expected to happen. Keep a neutral face and don't give verbal confirmations or detractions. Don't let the user feel like there's a right and wrong answer, even if there is, because you can learn from how they prefer to interact. Make sure to use follow-up questions such as "what did you expect to happen?" and "what were your top two things you liked and disliked about this experience?". The goal at the end of the session is to get the user talking about the experience overall.

Conduct the test with at least 4–8 people minimum (as suggested by *Just Enough Research*). This number gives you enough information to start spotting patterns. However, if patterns don't appear in the results, and different users had much different reactions, add in a few more tests for confirmation.

Synthesize the notes you took from all of the tests, and group them into categories of similar concerns or issues the user had. Address each category and determine what insight it gives you. How can you solve the issues that came up? Brainstorm a few different ways to solve the new problems, and repeat this entire process with a new prototype and research plan to test your new assumption.

For Tempo, I tested the prototype with a variety of different people who fit my user profile (Figure 4-26). I tried to get different age ranges and professions to give feedback. I also did a few intercept interviews at a local yoga meetup, because I needed feedback from additional people outside of my network.

FIGURE 4-26
User testing the Tempo prototype

The feedback I got was very helpful and promising. The two dials made sense to most users, and they were able to adjust the patterns based on the tasks that I posed them. I focused on different activities that would have a certain pace, and the user had to change the pattern to fit that use. I asked them how they would use the device in their daily lives, and got many different answers that opened up new possible use cases for the devices. Two of the more surprising uses were as a carpal tunnel massage sleeve, to alleviate pain, and as a silent metronome for playing drums. Other uses were for meditation, yoga, running pace, and presentation pace.

I received feedback on the feel of the vibration motors (sometimes too strong) and the lack of fine-tooth control with the type of dials that were on the prototype. Based on these results, I designed a more specific band that could be used for sports-based activities or for everyday use Additionally, I began designing the smartphone app that would make it easier to adjust and save certain patterns that the user liked most. After this round of prototyping, I combined what I learned with my previous assumptions, and determined the next round of design and testing that I needed to do.

Process in Action—An Etsy Case Study

Now that you've read about the different processes you can employ when prototyping, I'll take you through an example of that process in action. Etsy is an online marketplace for handmade goods, vintage wares, and supplies. They facilitate online and in-person sales around the world, and currently employ over 900 people including designers and engineers.

As Etsy's marketplace matures, the company wants to branch out and diversify their offerings. I spoke with an Etsy product team about their prototyping process for a recent project that culminated in the launch of a new part of the business. Kuan Luo, Senior Product Designer, and her team took on the task of designing a new product called Pattern, a custom website building tool for Etsy sellers (Figure 4-27).

The target users for Pattern are Etsy sellers who have a shop but don't yet have their own personal website. Kuan's team assumed part of this issue was due to time constraint and technical know-how. They began with user research in order to validate those assumptions and to better understand the real problems these users have. Kuan, along with the research team, conducted interviews with many different types of Etsy sellers. She visited them in their studios for contextual inquiry to get

a good feel for their brand and aesthetic (Figure 4-28). Her team additionally took into account Etsy's seller demographics to understand the
larger population of sellers.

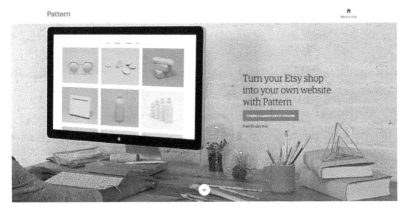

FIGURE 4-27
Pattern, Etsy's custom website building tool

FIGURE 4-28
The research team visited sellers' studios to get a feel for their brands and
aesthetics

Kuan and her product team already knew that the majority of sellers are women who use Etsy as a partial income. The major insights from interviewing sellers was that time is their scarcest resource, and that they wanted more control over the brand feel of their shop and website. This validated their first assumption that time constraint was a major issue, and illuminated a new pain point of brand aesthetics. Etsy's existing shop pages have few customizable areas, and the website itself has its own brand aesthetic. This style is simple, clean, and bright orange and white, but doesn't always fit what sellers imagine or prefer for their personal brand aesthetic.

One interviewee was a woman who sells handmade leather jackets and has a very dark, gothic brand (Figure 4-29). Etsy doesn't fit her brand style, and she wished she could have more of a say for how her shop looks and feels. She doesn't want to leave Etsy because she enjoys the exposure that the website brings her work. But the brand image was a pain point for her use of the marketplace.

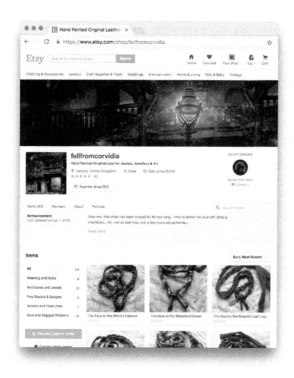

FIGURE 4-29

An example of a shop with a unique brand aesthetic

Based on this research, the product team began to design a website-building tool that would be easy and quick to use, but allow for a certain level of customization for individual brands. Kuan started by writing out initial user flows, to think through what scope the team should work on (Figure 4-30). With only a 10-person team working on the project to begin with, they had the difficult task of determining how to test the idea without allowing the scope to get out of hand. The team chose not to compete with custom website building companies like Squarespace, but they did want to provide tools for their very specific users.

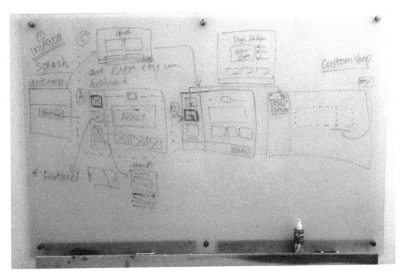

FIGURE 4-30
Kuan created an initial user flow to determine the scope of her prototypes

The user flow begins with the user learning about Pattern in a banner on Etsy.com and clicking it, and goes until the user completes her website setup. Once the user's steps were written, Kuan went back through the flow to design the interface for the different parts such as choosing a website theme and colors. Based on the interviews and researching competitors, she determined the top four features needed for the user to reach her goal were: overall themes, customization options, a custom domain, and allowing changes to the page content, starting with the about page and allowing listing changes in the future. The tool pulls most of the content from the existing product listings, making it fast to create the website, and will allow the user to edit and update that content in the website-building tool in a future release.

Kuan made paper mock-ups and wireframes to think through the layouts quickly (Figure 4-31). Then she jumped into a combination of Sketch and InVision to build and test interactive wireframes. She received feedback from her teammates often to help improve the design before user testing.

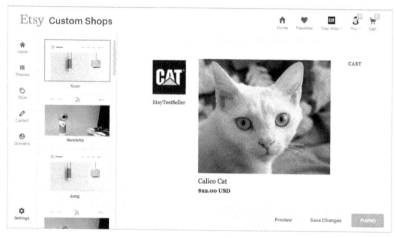

FIGURE 4-31

Kuan tested a mid-fidelity prototype with sellers to get feedback

Kuan doesn't use low-fidelity prototypes with sellers because the website-building tool required a lot of written content to support and allow the user to know what to do. She built a mid-fidelity clickable prototype to get feedback on how the customization and templates worked (Figure 4-32). In the prototype she included text and copy to help her user understand the flow of the interface. She was able to do three or four rounds of user testing with iterative improvements throughout the project.

One surprising insight she gained from testing was the level of customization that the sellers wanted. Originally, the product team assumed that giving more customization control to the user would result in unflattering website designs. They pared back the color choices and themes to limit how much customization could happen, and to maintain a certain level of aesthetic control. However, based on the feedback, sellers wanted to have full control over the website's aesthetics, even if it meant that some custom websites would have untraditional color combinations.

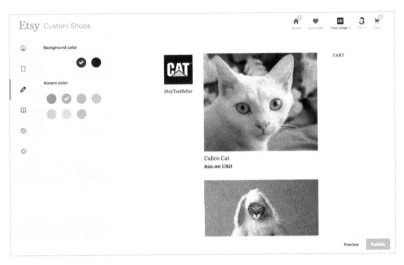

FIGURE 4-32

Kuan tested a limited color picker to see if sellers appreciated that additional feature

Kuan's team realized that it was more important for the user to have control over their full brand experience within this custom website, especially since it was a separate interface from Etsy's website. After that round of user testing, the team added a custom color picker to allow sellers to control their full brand customization (Figure 4-33).

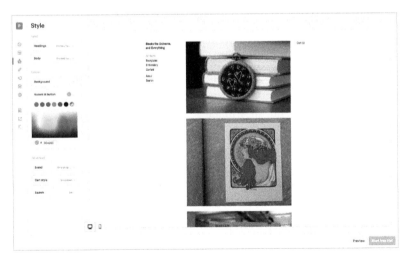

FIGURE 4-33

The final color picker is a huge success

The product team launched Pattern in April 2016 (Figure 4-34). They had quick adoption and success with their new product and hit their one-year goal within two months of the product launch. If Kuan were able to do it again, she would want to have more designers involved at the beginning of the project. That way she would have gotten help with the research and initial designs so the team could cover more ground. She would have additionally focused in on a few more detailed interactions and conducted A/B tests.

FIGURE 4-34

In the final Pattern setup, the user chooses a them for their website

By following a user-centered prototyping process, Kuan's product team was able to conduct quick, iterative tests of their website design tool. They were able to catch a major issue of customization before the product shipped that might have prevented users from signing up for the new service. In the end, they made a better experience for their users, and their product has been more successful for that effort (Figures 4-35 and 4-36).

FIGURE 4-35

The Pattern Dashboard gives recommendations and a simple onboarding
message

FIGURE 4-36

A sample Pattern website

Summary

The process of prototyping is very similar, but different, depending on your reason for prototyping, the goal, and your audience. By deciding on these three elements, you can use this section as a guide to help you figure out what you need to do and in what order. To get started quickly, make a "minimum viable prototype" to become more comfortable with prototyping. I use each of the other processes during the rest of my product development. Exploration comes early on before the concept is solidified, in order to think through alternatives and to confirm you're solving the right problem. Testing assumptions happens on and off throughout the development to test the ideas with real users. And you can present your findings and ideas through prototypes to your whole team in order to gain alignment and to agree on the proper direction for the project.

With each of these different processes, your can focus on what's necessary and efficiently manage your work.

Prototyping for Digital Products

Software and app design are a huge opportunity area for directly impacting people. The internet and the active open source community has democratized software development. It's easy to get started, and with merely a text editor, you can prototype interactive, engaging experiences. To take it one step further, a collaborative team can create useful products that can be scaled for mass use. By prototyping your digital product, you'll learn how to improve your idea, and make it the next big hit, whether you're at a startup or a well-established company.

The focus of this chapter is how to prototype for screen-based interactions and the larger experiences that include them. I won't be covering how to code and implement designs, but I will give you actionable ways to prototype experiences and communicate design intentions to business stakeholders and developers.

Getting Started with Digital

The best way to get started in software design is to find a user need and to jump into solving it. The need can be something that seems silly, such as knowing exactly when it starts raining at your house, and building a smartphone app solution that notifies you if it detects rain outside. But by having an idea that solves a problem, you'll have assumptions to test, and a good idea of where to start prototyping.

SCOPING

A hard part about prototyping for digital products is preventing scope and feature creep of the product and the prototype. That means actively trying not to solve too many things with one interface, and not allowing business stakeholders to add new features at late points in the process. If anything, as you test your product idea, you should be able to pare down the features and interactions until you've created the core experience. You might need to advocate for the user in order to prevent last-minute additions. In order to support your designs and direction, make sure to document your user research and test it well to use as backup.

To give one example, the team that created Sketch focused on software to make user interface design easier. They tried to solve pain points designers have with existing products such as Adobe's Illustrator and Photoshop (Figure 5-1). Both of those products were created for traditional print and graphic design work, but have since been adopted to design interfaces too. Software designers were frustrated with the speed of Illustrator and the layering system of Photoshop; neither was the right fit of features they needed to complete their work quickly.

FIGURE 5-1
Sketch purposefully scoped their software design to tackle the largest pain points of their main competitor, Illustrator

Sketch's design team learned exactly what tools and support designers needed to make screen design faster and easier. They made symbols, which allow a user to make changes in one place to update the symbol throughout the entire document (Figure 5-2). Sketch also made a new file type that saves faster and imports into many different prototyping and animation programs.

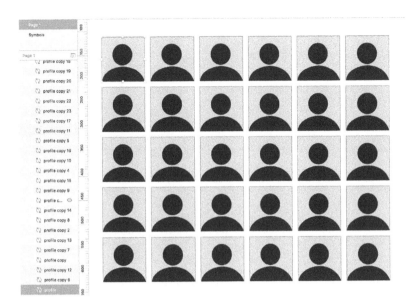

FIGURE 5-2

Symbols allow a designer to make one element and reuse it across a
document, with the ability to update them all at the same time

Instead of building out additional features, they encouraged their community to make open source plugins to do more functional heavy lifting. One example is the Craft plugin, created by InVision, that provides many functions like duplicating, real fake data, and syncing
with InVision itself (Figure 5-3). By allowing these other companies to
build extra features, Sketch's product itself didn't get too bloated, and
users could decide what extra features they wanted to install. Their
final product makes it faster to create screen mock-ups and to make
them into prototypes with secondary software. By disrupting the typical design software industry, Sketch is improving the entire market by
helping other companies improve their product design and experience.

FIGURE 5-3

Craft is a plugin for
Sketch that gives
designers extra
features like data,
duplication, and
syncing with InVision

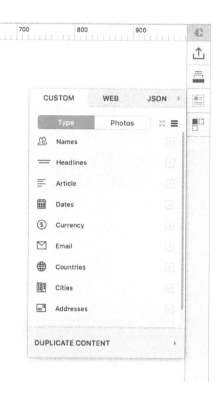

What's Unique for Digital

Digital products have their own set of essential characteristics. Their design is mostly based on the screen interactions and the varying sizes and input methods for our current devices. Some of the unique aspects of designing digital products include screens, responsive design, different interaction types, accessibility, and animations.

SCREENS

What makes software different than hardware is the fact that it's delivered via a device with a screen rather than as a standalone, physical product (Figure 5-4). If you're designing a smart object that has a screen input/output, you can refer to this chapter to design those interactions. Screens are amazing in their ability to transfer information, allowing us to connect to the internet and to one another. The software that we use to create our designs was itself designed and coded within the same interface.

FIGURE 5-4
Digital products are
delivered through a
screen

As interaction designers, we get firsthand experience using our medium on a daily basis. You should use that time to always be observing and learning about new interaction patterns and design elements. But it can be easy to get distracted by the plethora of poor user experiences within apps and applications. If you find a frustrating experience, think through different ways to improve it and bring that thoughtful analysis to your actual work.

Also, whenever you use a screen-based program or website, ask yourself if you know where you are and where you can go next. Navigation is a huge element of screen-based flows, and understanding how to indicate where the user is and is going will be helpful to your everyday work.

Screens have limitations too. There is a limited amount of interaction space due to the screen size and being two dimensional. You can *indicate* three dimensions in an interface, but until we're designing for virtual or augmented reality interfaces, we can only fake the indication of depth in our designs. There are quite a few options for faking it, though. You can incorporate depth by using a z-index for your coded interactions, which layers elements in front or behind each other (Figure 5-5). And you can layer your interface like Google's Material Design system does to indicate depth and importance of elements (Figure 5-6).

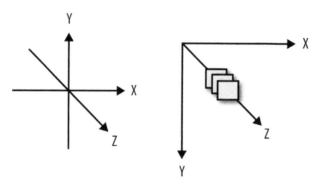

FIGURE 5-5

You can design on the x, y, and z indexes

FIGURE 5-6

Google Material Design
utilizes layering to
indicate depth

Do.

Softer, larger shadows indicate the floating action button is at
a higher elevation than the blue sheet, which has a crisper
shadow.

When you prototype for screen-based interactions, it's best to simulate the actual screen, in shape, size, or medium. The final medium of digital products is code rendered in a browser or on a desktop. You must test your ideas in this actual medium during your process, but until you're ready to code a more refined version of your idea, you can simulate the screen through paper or other means.

RESPONSIVE DESIGN

When you're designing computer software or enterprise-level software, you know that there is a specific setting that programs will be used in—a computer on a desk or lap, and usually in an office. But if your software or application is hosted on the web, it can not only be used on *any* device, but in almost any situation that one can use a smartphone.

If you're designing a web-based digital experience or a smartphone app, you must design it to be mobile-first and responsive. Smartphone browsing has exponentially increased in the last few years, and surpassed desktop browsing in 2014.[1] With this in mind, it's crucial to create prototypes for a variety of screen sizes, and even better to create responsive prototypes that you can use to test both the desktop and mobile experience.

Mobile-first design means thinking through how your product will be used on the smallest screen size possible and the constraints that come with that medium. Mobile browsers don't have access to all of the third-party plug-ins you might be used to on desktop. Your goal is to design the best experience for small-screen usage, and then slowly enhance that experience as it scales to larger sizes.

It might seem similar to start with desktop and pare down the design until it works for a smaller screen, but that process is a graceful degradation instead of enhancement. It is obvious to the user that the mobile "version" is a secondary thought. That's why we have so many crappy mobile websites! There's usually less time devoted to making the best experience, and after you've built out an interface that depends on specific plug-ins, there's often not an alternative version available for mobile browsers.

By reframing the problem from degradation to enhancement, you're focused on making the best experience with the most constraints first, which results in better designs. Only then can you add in extra, superfluous features and functions when they become available in desktop browsers. Or you might find that this exercise creates a better, more focused product and end up leaving out the extra features that don't

1   Mary Meeker, "2015 Internet Trends Report," 2015 Internet Trends—Kleiner Perkins Caufield Byers, May 27, 2015, accessed January 10, 2016, *http://www.kpcb.com/ internettrends*.

work on mobile screens. Either way, you'll be prototyping and making the best product for your users, no matter which device they use to access your product. (Figure 5-7)

Graceful Degradation

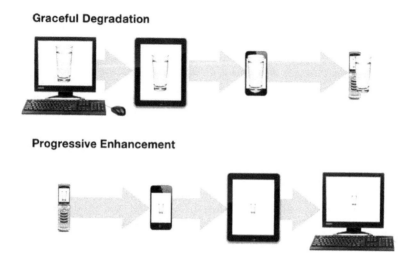

Progressive Enhancement

FIGURE 5-7

Desktop-first graceful degradation versus mobile-first progressive enhancement (image courtesy of Brad Frost)

Responsive design means that as you increase the browser window or device size, the layout and design will change slightly to look and work the best at every screen size (Figure 5-8). To do this, you must choose breakpoints where, as you increase the size, the design breaks and looks terrible. At each breakpoint, you make minor changes to the layout of the design in order to have a good experience on any device. When you decide your breakpoints, try building and testing prototypes for each one. That way, you can make sure that your arrangement works no matter the screen size.

For more information on both these points, check out *Mobile First* by Luke Wroblewski and *Responsive Web Design* by Ethan Marcotte (A Book Apart).

FIGURE 5-8

Responsive design creates breakpoints when needed and alters the layout to work the best at all sizes

Try not to use "standard breakpoints" for mobile, tablet, and desktop. This idea of three standard sizes is false, as there are hundreds of different screen sizes within each of those categories (Figure 5-9), and two different orientations for mobile and tablet. Instead, by scaling the browser size and choosing the proper breakpoints for your product, you'll ensure a good experience no matter what device the user has.

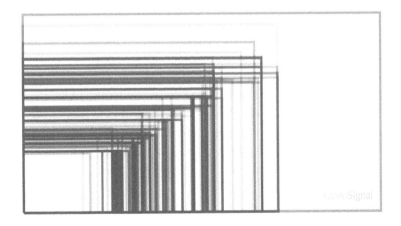

FIGURE 5-9

These rectangles indicate the screen sizes for just Android products (image courtesy of OpenSignal)

Additionally, responsive design pertains to the information you show, and the types of interactions you include. As your screen real estate grows, and you gain access to browser plug-ins, you might be able to do more interesting motions and interactions (Figure 5-10). The goal is not to withhold any content or interactions from small-screen users, but to create the full experience for them, and add additional aspects as needed to larger screen sizes.

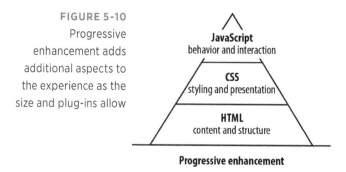

FIGURE 5-10

Progressive enhancement adds additional aspects to the experience as the size and plug-ins allow

You'll need to prototype and test your breakpoints at a few different levels in order to best understand how your user will interact with it. For mid- to high-fidelity prototypes, it's easy to build out both a small screen and desktop version of your wireframes, and make them into quick clickable prototypes with a program like InVision.

A few additional considerations when designing for screens, and especially smaller screens, are typography and hover interactions. Your content must be legible on a smaller screen size, and the suggested minimum font size is 16px or 1em. By keeping your font size at or above that size, your users won't need to zoom in as often, and you'll have better control over how they view and interact with your designs. Also, there's not currently a way to hover in mobile, so make sure to think through alternative ways to display tooltips or contextual information. Instead of hover, use a click action to open and close tool tips. Make sure your buttons and clickable elements are distinguishable from static elements without using hover.

DESIGNING FOR DIFFERENT INTERACTION TYPES

With mobile and screen design comes the additional work of designing for touch and voice interactions. A great book to reference for touch-based design is Josh Clark's *Designing for Touch* (A Book Apart). He digs into the ergonomics of touch screens, sizing of elements, and how to make gestures intuitive and discoverable. To prototype and test these aspects of a design, you need to be a bit more crafty with your paper prototypes, or jump into software early on so that you can test on the real devices.

Here are some common gestures and how to accommodate them in a paper prototype (Figure 5-11):

Touch
> Normal click or select, such as buttons. Have clickable elements in a different color or underlined as links to indicate that they are indeed buttons or selectable items, then follow through with the action that they would set off.

Double touch, pinch open, and pinch closed
> Typically used for zooming. Have a zoomed in and zoomed out version of the portion of your screen that is zoomable. When the user double touches or pinches, switch out that portion.

Drag, swipe, or fling
> Causes scrolling or dismissing of a notification. Have a longer piece of paper you can pull through the viewing pane to indicate a longer page, and have your notifications layered on the prototype so you can easily pull them off.

Two-, three-, or four-finger swipe
> Can cause many different things. Decide what will happen and have additional screens for each scenario in case the user tries it.

Two-finger tap
> Typically zooms or opens "right-click menu" in macOS. See double touch for the zoom, or have the right-click menu available to put in frame if the user "right-clicks."

Two-finger press and rotate
> Have the element be separate in the frame so that you can rotate it, or let the user rotate it normally.

Hard touch (3D touch on iOS)
> Causes extra menus to open. Have a quick actions pop-up menu ready or content preview to put into frame upon hard touch.

Long press and swipe
> Pick up and move. Have any moveable object be separate pieces of paper that can be dragged around by the user.

Pull down at top

Choose what this action does for you, then show refresh screen (like Snapchat) or additional menu (like many websites).

Edge swipes

Have any menus or additional screens ready to go so that you can put them in frame.

FIGURE 5-11
You can test gestures at a low-fidelity level before you begin building out or coding them (image courtesy of Flickr user Rob Enslin)

With mobile, screen-based products, you have the opportunity to interact with voice input and audio output more easily than on a desktop. For example, if you're designing a conversational assistant, you can build prototypes of the conversation and visual displays of it (Figure 5-12). You can prototype these interactions with proxy speakers and play-testing in your tests.

In your user test, you can have the facilitator play the role of the assistant, reacting to user requests verbally, and then in real time, writing down the conversation on the paper interface to indicate how it will look as it populates the screen. At a lower fidelity, you can just have the user talk to you without a paper interface, and have a list of prompts they can choose from and predesigned responses that the assistant would provide. Either way, you're testing this new interaction type before investing too much time in building the actual conversation engine.

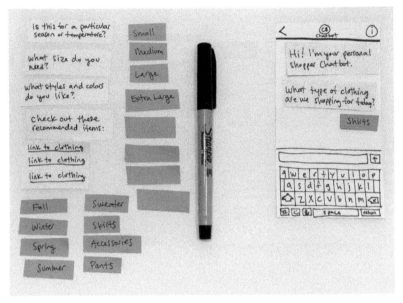

FIGURE 5-12

A conversational interface paper prototype

ACCESSIBILITY

You should consider all types of users when you're designing software, web apps, or smartphone apps. Accessibility refers to designing an interface that anyone can interact with, no matter the device or assistive technology they use or their ability level. Some common design considerations include users with visual, auditory, physical, speech, or cognitive impairment; users with color blindness; and users using assistive technology such as screen readers and keyboard-only inputs.

For visual impairment and color blindness, the consideration for your design and prototypes is to test your contrast ratios and color choices, which you can do using the contrast ratio tool (*http://bit.ly/2hMgVo6*), shown in Figure 5-13. Contrast ratio is a metric that compares the color of text to the background color it's viewed on. In order for low-vision and color-blind people to be able to read the content in your product, you need to ensure a high enough ratio. Font weight and size affect the contrast ratio too, so try not to use a low-contrast color on a thin font weight. Make sure to test this ratio for every prototype you make at a higher fidelity level. Don't wait until the end of your process to check, because you might have to rework your visual design.

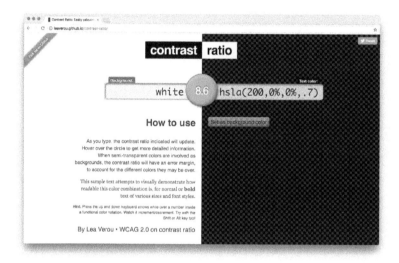

FIGURE 5-13
A contrast ratio tool to help with content accessibility

Color blindness specifically occurs in a green-type, red-type, and blue-type. The most common are green and red, and 8% of men worldwide have some form of color blindness. Fewer women do; about 4.5% of the entire world population have it.[2] Try to avoid a few color combinations that directly affect those with color blindness; especially green and red, green and brown, blue and purple, and green and blue (Figure 5-14). Include a few users with color blindness or visual impairment in your user testing, especially at higher fidelity levels. They will be able to point out issues that are hidden in plain sight.

---

2   We Are Colorblind, "A quick introduction to colorblindness," http://bit.ly/2gQYfTW.

| Normal vision | Deuteran | Protan |

FIGURE 5-14
"Normal" vision versus green/red and blue/yellow color blindness

Screen readers and keyboard-only inputs are another specific way that users interact with software. A screen reader converts the text and images of your page into synthesized speech and outputs it as audio. It may be used by someone who is blind, or heavily vision-impaired. At least a few times in your prototyping process, especially when you're making coded prototypes, run it through a screen reader to hear how some of your users will interact with your product.

Keyboard-only inputs are usually used due to physical impairments that do not allow the ability to use a mouse. Instead, users navigate an interface with the arrow keys or the tab button on a keyboard. The best way to ensure a good experience for both screen readers and keyboard input interaction types is to make sure your developer is using appropriate document structuring. Screen readers and keyboards navigate the document structure to find value for their users. If your developer creates clean code that is structured and has appropriate alternatives for image content, your users will be better supported.

There are many best practices for how to design and code for all ability levels. You should read through the technical standards on the Web Accessibility Toolkit (*http://bit.ly/2gPEhZu*). It is helpful to user test with people of all ability levels to ensure your design is universally accessible. If you aren't able to incorporate actual people, at least simulate and test your prototypes based on these best practices.

Apple and Android include accessibility tools in their operating systems to allow for screen reading and increasing contrast and font sizes. Try turning these on to test your coded designs, and to ensure your design can be understood by all types of users. To access this menu on an Apple computer, go to System Preferences→Accessibility. On iOS, go to Settings→General→Accessibility (Figure 5-15). For Android, it's Settings→Accessibility.

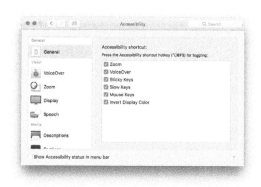

FIGURE 5-15
Accessibility menu on Apple desktop and mobile

ANIMATIONS

Both physical and digital products have many interactive elements to test, but animation and motion are a necessary consideration for digital products specifically. Motion in an interface adds context and overall ease of understanding for users. It connects user actions to the system's outcomes, creating behavior definition and choreography through the experience. As users move through your product, they can interpret motion as the intuitive body language of your design. It helps your users build their mental model of the product and adds personality to reinforce the brand identity. The motion that occurs between two screens is an opportunity to direct your user to the most important aspect of the next page.

It's vital to prototype and test animations because they may require more engineering effort than other parts of the interface (Figure 5-16). You need to be sure that the motion is adding value to the user's experience and understanding before you invest your developers' time into making it a reality.

FIGURE 5-16
It's important to prototype animations early to give developers time to build them

You can prototype and communicate animations in many ways. The easiest way to create and test animations is to do a quick storyboard to think through the different states (Figure 5-17). What happens in between the two screens when you tap a call to action? You can use this simple sketch to talk with developers about feasibility to code the specific motion. However, you might find that your team needs a better understanding of how the motion looks and acts.

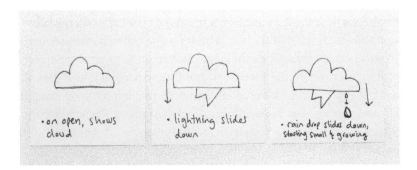

FIGURE 5-17
Animation storyboards are a good way to communicate your intent easily with little skill needed

You can make mid-fidelity motion prototypes by using software like Keynote. It may be surprising that a presentation software has been hacked to create UI animations, but it's an easy way to play and try out animations without investing too much time. Keynote has many motions built in, and the ability to create your own (Figure 5-18).

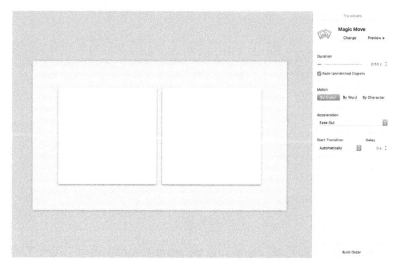

FIGURE 5-18
You can build motion prototypes in Keynote

For most animations in Keynote, all you need is a start and end position, then Magic Move will automatically make the motion between states. You can adjust the scale, position, and rotation of the elements, and you can customize the duration and acceleration of the motion. By using ease in and out, your motion will come off as smoother, and you won't be able to tell that it's from a presentation software. You can even create clickable prototypes that you can use on your smartphone by adding links within the document, and then exporting it to HTML. It will not export production code that you can use, but it's good enough for user testing. For more information about using Keynote for animations, check out the tutorial "How to Prototype UI Animations in Keynote" from *Smashing Mag* (*http://bit.ly/2gPCF1W*).

You can make higher-fidelity animations with specific software, and save videos of the animations for testing or communication. Some current animation prototyping tools include Flinto, Framer, Pixate, Motion by InVision, and Principle (Figure 5-19). There seems to be a new tool every day that allows you to animate your design files into a full user experience. You can import your mid- to high-fidelity wireframes from Sketch, Photoshop, or Illustrator and animate them with built-in, customizable motions. Or you can build low-fidelity wireframes with the program's basic drawing tools to try out motion before committing to it. Framer is a bit different because it's code-based for producing high-fidelity animation. But you can still use Sketch files if they're organized properly.

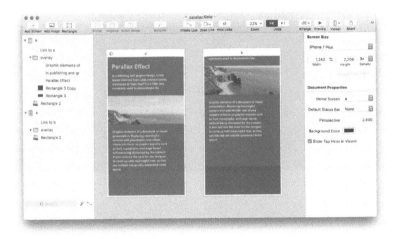

FIGURE 5-19

For more complex animations or motion at a high fidelity, try using Flinto (shown here), Framer, or Principle

If you're really interested in motion design, try using a more powerful tool like AfterEffects to build in-depth timelines and intricate motion (Figure 5-20). You can then translate those motions into coded animations with CSS. You can export SVGs, a type of vector image, of specific graphics and manipulate them with CSS so that they animate and move. This type of animation is better for loading indicators and icon-based motion. Once you get more comfortable with animations, you can code most of them straight into your high-fidelity prototypes. Many motions can be created with CSS, making them lighter on performance (since they don't need images) and faster to load.

When you have animations integrated in your prototype for user testing, pay attention to how it directs the user through the interface. Is the motion giving the user proper context, or is it distracting them from their task? Watch how the different pages scroll up or in from a side. Does that motion maintain the user's sense of location? When you're user testing, see if the user understands where they are spatially within your app or software.

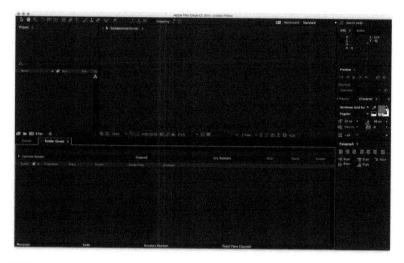

FIGURE 5-20

AfterEffects is a powerful tool for creating custom animation or motion studies

All of these different aspects of motion—context, loading, and personality—are areas you can prototype and test in a mid- to high-fidelity prototype. Ensure you're making informed decisions instead of making pretty animations. Even the most beautiful animation can derail an experience if it's not applied and used properly.

Be judicious in your application of animation and motion. Ensure that each movement has a purpose and is contributing to the overall user experience in a positive way. For a more detailed dive into motion design, check out Val Head's *Designing Interface Animation* (Rosenfeld).

Preparation

With just a few basic assets, you can focus your prototype and ensure it's covering what you need and contributing to your overall process. Take the time to prepare by creating your user flow and sketching out a variety of ways to accommodate that flow.

USER FLOW

A *user flow* is how someone moves through using your software or app, navigating the different screens to accomplish their goal. When you've decided on a pain point, you can then think of a few different ways to solve it through user flows. Based on the user's goal, design a "happy path," or the route that is the easiest and fastest way for a user to complete her or his task.

When you've created a happy path, you must prototype and test it in order to confirm that the navigation is clear and is the most intuitive way for your user to navigate. Oftentimes, a user will find a new way to move through your app and might miss some functions because of that. By testing prototypes, you'll be able to improve the overall design to help the user move from task to task.

User flows are a great way to scope your prototype. You can write out an entire flow for a specific user, then choose which parts of the flow are most assumption-based. You'll find that breaking a complex interaction down into smaller chunks allows you to move faster and test more of the intricate interactions instead of doing a high-level, overarching test.

For example, if I'm designing a social media app where people post interesting sounds that they hear, I might create a user flow that looks something like Figure 5-21.

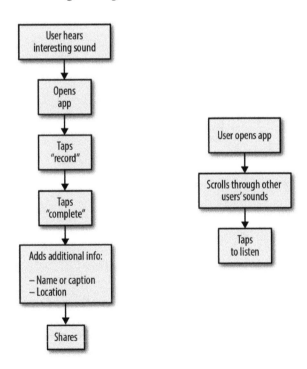

FIGURE 5-21

A user flow for a sound-based social media app

I then look for the riskiest, assumption-based parts of the user flow so that I can quickly target and test those aspects. For my sound social media, I need to start by testing the recording and sharing process (Figure 5-22). Once I get that part of the app designed and tested, I can go back to the other, more standard parts, such as the log in or the profile. By tackling the riskiest part first, I can ensure my team is on the right track, and pivot quickly if we aren't.

User flows aren't merely a prioritization tool, they're great preparation for prototyping. By having a written user flow, either in words, a diagram, or as a storyboard, you can determine the type of interactions you need to design and prototype later.

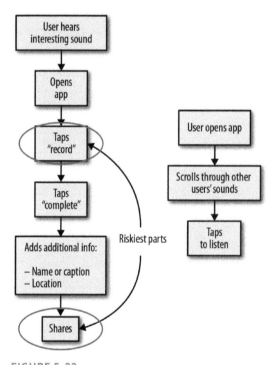

FIGURE 5-22
Now I can scope my prototype to a specific part of the user flow

Start with how the user finds your product and write out the flow until they are finished using it. Write out each step that the user will take to complete their task in your app. If you write this out on Post-its, you can think through alternative flows by reordering them and moving them around. This exercise helps you be flexible with the interface you design.

Create multiple user flows for different types of users. You might have a few personas to work through. At the very least, you will have a first-time user and a return user. For example, your sign-in interaction will be different for these users, and a first-time user might need an onboarding experience that a return user does not (Figure 5-23).

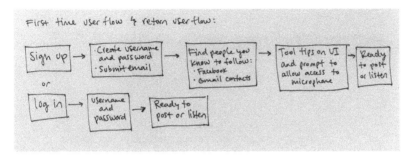

FIGURE 5-23
Draw out how a first time user and a return user would interact with your product

You can iterate on the user flow by showing it to your team and business stakeholders to get feedback on the use of the product. At this point, you might even be able to get some feasibility feedback from developers. Keep your whole team in the loop as you work through these initial phases, so that you stay aligned about the product you are creating.

SKETCHES

Now that you have a core idea for the flow of your app, you can begin to draw out the interface your user needs to accomplish their goals. Go through each step of your user flow and sketch out the different components and a few ideas of how they will be organized (Figure 5-24). You can iterate on these sketches by drawing lots of variations to think of alternative ways to solve the same interaction pattern. Check out Chapter 4's exploration-centric process for more guidance on ideation and prioritization of directions.

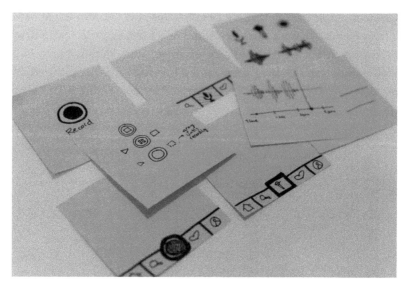

Iterate on your idea through sketches or mock-ups

Low-Fidelity Digital Prototypes

It's best to begin prototyping with a lower fidelity in order to think through large concepts before committing to a specific direction. One area you need to work out at a broader level is the information architecture (IA), or how the interface is organized and labeled (Figure 5-25). IA and wireframing might seem more like preparation for actual, interactive prototypes, but I've purposely placed them in this section because they are testable. If you create user tests for your IA and wireframes before putting time into a more elaborate interaction, you can answer some big questions. IA not only deals with organization, it determines what terminology a user best understands. Wireframes allow you to visualize how you might translate that IA into an interface. Both are valuable to test before moving on to more interactive methods.

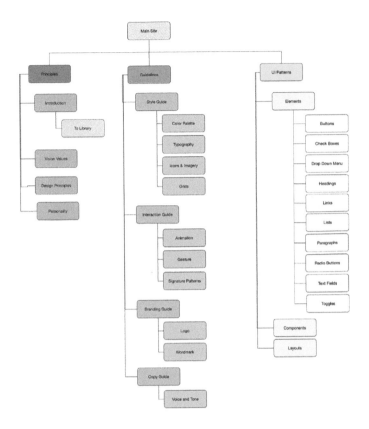

FIGURE 5-25
You can test information architecture for organization and terminology

Other low-fidelity prototypes include paper prototypes (Figure 5-26) and clickable prototypes. Both are easy to make and require little skill or time. If you have Post-its or paper lying around, you can create a simple version of your interface to test. You might not want to use these prototypes for communication or advocating (see Chapter 2), but they can be used to discuss general concepts at a high level. Business stakeholders and development teams won't have enough context to understand specific design interactions. Try using a mid- to high-fidelity prototype instead.

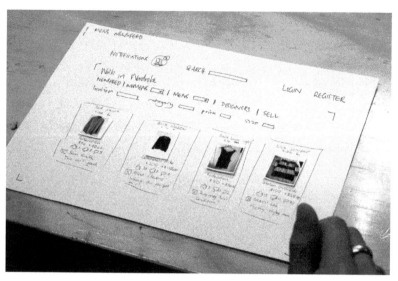

FIGURE 5-26

Paper prototypes are a great way to get started prototyping for digital products (photo courtesy of Flickr user Samuel Mann)

INFORMATION ARCHITECTURE

If your product has navigation, content, or terminology (pretty much any product) then you have the responsibility to develop the information architecture. IA is the structure of your software or app. Your goal for IA is to create the most intuitive labels, groupings, categories, and site map for your user (Figure 5-27). Think through what kind of data and information will be distributed in your digital product. If you already have content, use it in your prototype. If you don't have content yet, try to write something along the lines of what you expect to have. That way when you test, you can get a better understanding of how the user navigates through your product with text-based context.

Your user might be used to different terminology based on their domain or the type of software you're making. An informal social media app will have different terminology and navigation than an enterprise-level medical software. You might not know the type of terminology your user prefers. Learn from them directly by interviewing them and hearing vocabulary they use in their daily work.

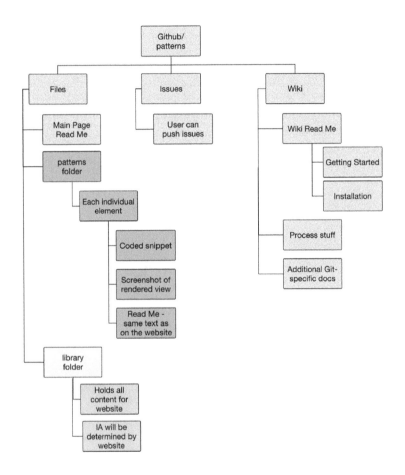

Github & Website Codependencies

FIGURE 5-27
Your IA includes labels, groupings, categories, and site maps

You can perform a card-sorting activity to understand how your user naturally groups different items or terms (Figure 5-28). Write each term, page, or section of a page onto a separate card (depending on the scope of your test). Write a card for each category and subcategory or section label you assume you'll need (such as home, contact, profile, cart, etc.). Include a few blank cards and a pen so that the user can write additional categories or terms. Give your user the stack of mixed-up cards, and ask them to sort them into logical groupings and assign a category name to each grouping. Tell them that there's no right answer, so that they're not looking to you for clues. You're trying to get their unbiased understanding of where they would expect to find these aspects of your product. This version of card sorting is a closed method, where you're prescribing the names of categories for the user to organize.

An open version of this test holds back the category names, and first has the user write down their own categories. That way you can see if they use different wordings than what you previously wrote out. You'll get a good idea of your user's mental model and any additional wordings that you might not have thought of yourself.

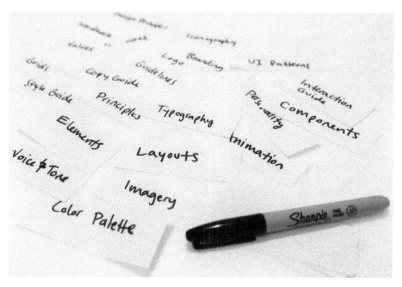

FIGURE 5-28
A card sort helps test the IA of a product

Additionally, you can test IA through sitemaps and clickable prototypes, which I cover later in this chapter. Sitemaps are a good way to communicate organization without showing low-fidelity prototypes, or when you test your clickable prototype, observe how your user navigates through the product, and keep an eye out for when they get confused about the location of information or how things are labeled. If a user gets lost, ask them what they expected to find. Take that information into account when you revisit the navigation design and information organization. For an deeper dive into IA, check out *How to Make Sense of Any Mess* by Abby Covert and *Information Architecture for the World Wide Web* by Peter Morville and Louis Rosenfeld (O'Reilly).

WIREFRAMES

Information architecture and sketches quickly evolve into wireframes (Figure 5-29). *Wireframes* are a static layout of the pages of a digital product. They force you to think through placement of the different elements on a screen, and allow you to better visualize your IA. Wireframes start as low fidelity so that detailed visual design (like colors and specific typography) don't distract from the initial planning phase. Most designers use grayscale and placeholder boxes to indicate content in order to set expectations about where they are in their design process.

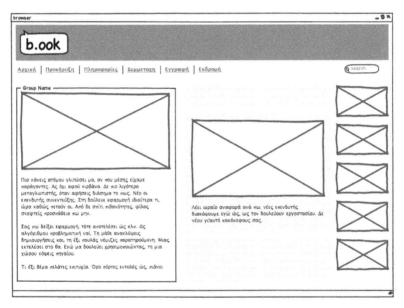

FIGURE 5-29
A basic wireframe

Wireframing is a great way to think about all of your interactions and communicate them in two dimensions. Draw out, on Post-its, paper, or in a program, each of your pages and screens. Make sure to create a few breakpoint wireframes with small screen and medium screen sizes. If you're building mobile-first, draw out the small screen size first. Otherwise, work on multiple sizes at this stage simultaneously to help you understand how the interface may be responsive.

I usually start with Post-its because it forces me to think at a small screen size (Figure 5-30). Once I have the entire interface drawn out with Post-its, I either make a fast clickable prototype, or I translate it into the computer as both small screen and large screen sizes.

FIGURE 5-30

I start with Post-it wireframes to think through high-level elements and placement

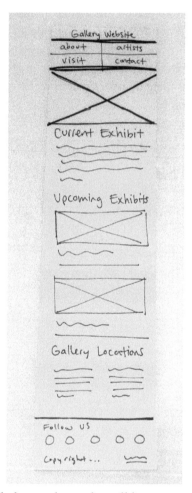

At the wireframing stage, you should choose the grid you'll be using, since you're already making design decisions around the layout and organization of the pages (Figure 5-31). Work with your content strategist and developers to understand how much text to expect on each page and what frameworks they currently use, and choose a grid that will work within those constraints and for your users. By choosing a grid early in your process, you can build your design around a base structure instead of willy-nilly, and lessen the risk that you will need to overhaul a design later on in your process. If you don't take an active part in choosing a grid, someone else will, and it might not work with your designs. As you create the full picture of your software, test it with your colleagues to see if your layout and organization make sense to other people. You can take the time to conduct A/B tests to compare alternative design concepts. The more feedback loops you create in your process, the better your product will be.

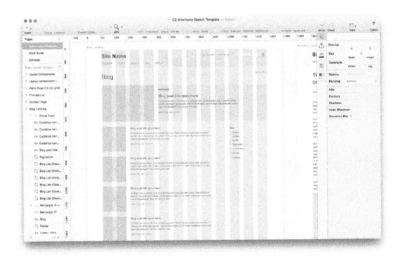

FIGURE 5-31
Choosing a grid early on will help you keep a consistent structure and make it easier for your developer to code your design

Make higher-fidelity wireframes by adding more of the final content, or adding visual design. However, you can skip the high-fidelity wireframes if you or your developer can jump straight into HTML/CSS and code in-browser. Some developers require high-fidelity wireframes with redlines (an overlay of dimensions and pixel-perfect numbers to implement), but redlines often stagnate the process, making it take longer to accomplish less (Figure 5-32). Invite your developer to do *pair design*, where you work side by side to finalize the wireframes and design as it's being implemented in code. It's faster to make minor tweaks, and allows you to work more efficiently.

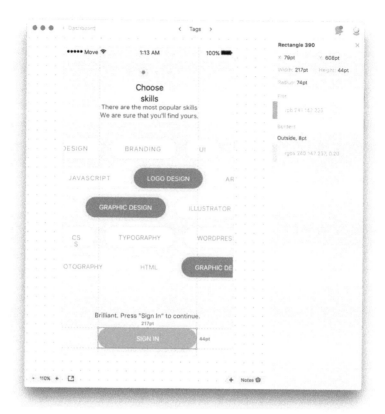

FIGURE 5-32

High-fidelity wireframes can include redlines to help developers know exactly what spacing and colors you've specified

PAPER PROTOTYPES

Paper prototypes are the easiest prototype to make for digital products. They're low fidelity, low cost, and low skill. They make it easy to quickly go from idea to test, and enable you to try out many different ways to solve the same problem in a short amount of time. If you already have your wireframes drawn, making it into a prototype takes even less time; you can print your wireframes and be ready to go!

To make a paper prototype, think back to your user flow or a specific assumption you want to test (navigation, completing a partial task, etc.) in order to decide which parts of the design will be needed. Draw out each screen on separate pieces of paper or Post-its, with each interaction having an additional piece of paper (Figure 5-33). You can even cut out buttons in different colors to indicate what's clickable or to better show what happens when you click a button.

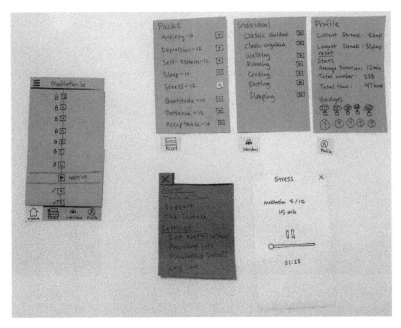

FIGURE 5-33
All the pages in a paper prototype

One potential pitfall of paper prototypes is that the user might not have enough context to make their way through. That's why it's helpful to include real content so that your test doesn't give you false feedback due to the lack of context in your design.

When you test your paper prototype (Figure 5-34), set expectations for the user that this is a very early version and needs high-level feedback. Arrange your screen pages so that you can switch them out as the user "clicks" on the prototype. But don't allow the user to see too much of the other pages—you don't want them to accidentally cheat. It might be awkward the first couple times, but you'll get better at orchestrating all the pages and interactive pieces of your prototype.

Pose the task to the user, and ask them to use the paper prototype to navigate and complete the task. As they "click" on different buttons, or pose questions, take the appropriate action that the interface would do. Don't give away too much additional information. If a user wants to go down an unexpected path, let them try, and ask them what they expected to be able to do.

FIGURE 5-34
You must orchestrate the test in order to properly move the paper prototype based on the user's interactions

Users can get frustrated by this type of interaction; paper is not the same as a screen. Some users can't imagine the paper as a device. When you go through their quotes to find insights later on, make sure to take out anything directly referencing the medium of the prototype.

You can make different fidelities of paper prototypes depending on your goal for testing. Review the five dimensions of fidelity (Chapter 3), and choose which ones are most appropriate. Paper prototypes will always have pretty low visual and interactive fidelity due to the medium. However, you can increase the visual fidelity by designing the interface in a software program and printing it out (Figure 5-35). You can build a prototype with higher fidelity of depth or breadth if your user flow or interaction require it. And you can always add more real, specific content so the user has context.

FIGURE 5-35
You can make higher-fidelity paper prototypes by designing the interface in
software and printing it out (image courtesy of Flickr user Priit Tammets)

By adding more content, more detailed buttons, and illustrations, you
can get feedback on all parts of your design. Try out alternative wordings for your calls to action, different sizes of buttons, and even completely different layouts for the same content. This step is where you
want to establish your core assumptions, and experiment while you
still have the opportunity to change them.

However, it might be just as easy to make a clickable prototype instead
of spending too much time on high-fidelity paper prototypes. It's different for each person and project, so decide which prototype is best
for your needs and process. Another downside of paper prototyping is
that you need to be in person to conduct the user testing. If you need to
test prototypes remotely, try making a low-fidelity clickable prototype
instead.

LOW-FIDELITY CLICKABLE PROTOTYPES
Another way to make a low-fidelity prototype is by turning your analog paper prototypes or digital wireframes into clickable prototypes.
Clickable prototypes automate the interactions within your interface
to make your prototype easier to interact with and test. Depending on

the software, this type of prototype can be as simple as adding hotspots on top of your hand-drawn wireframes. Or it can be more complex and higher-fidelity by incorporating aspects like drag and drop, animations, gestures, and more refined visuals.

Some of the current software and apps that make building clickable prototypes easy include Prototyping on Paper (PoP), InVision, Marvel, Proto.io, Axure, and UXPin (see Figure 5-36 and Table 5-1 for detailed information on some of the current tools). This category of software is exploding with new products to try every day. If you already have a good understanding of one of these softwares, go ahead and use it. If you're new to this type of product, don't get too stuck on choosing which one to learn and use. I recommend starting with PoP or InVision at first, because of their lower learning curve, and then look for alternatives when you need more functionality or a different type of prototyping— like complex interactions or motion design.

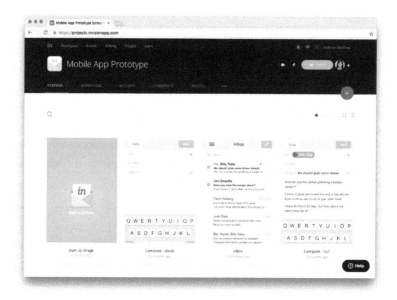

FIGURE 5-36
An example of a prototyping tool is InVision

TABLE 5-1. Overview of current technology you can use for prototyping and pros and cons for each. Most information courtesy of Emily Schwartzman and Cooper (*https://www.cooper.com/prototyping-tools*).

NAME OF PROGRAM	FIDELITY	USER TESTING	PROS	CONS
Axure	Medium-high	Average	Create complex interactions, works with any digital format, expansive library of widgets to build out screens	High learning curve, difficult to use existing mocks
Balsamiq	Low	Low	Quick, low-fidelity prototypes	Limited functionality and motion options
Framer	High	Average	High-fidelity animation and interactions, can import Sketch or Illustrator files	Code-based, steep learning curve
HotGloo	Low	Low	Good library of UI elements	No import options, no animation support
Indigo Studio	Medium	Average	Gesture-based interactions, can prototype any digital format	Doesn't import mock-ups, just images, moderate learning curve
InVision	Medium-high	Good	Easy to learn, great feedback and sharing system, easy to import from Sketch or Illustrator	No features for creating elements, must have file from other program, hotspots only
Justinmind	Medium	Good	Good animation and gesture tools, stimulates final device for testing	Moderate learning curve
Keynote	Medium	Medium	Low-skill animation prototyping	Limited functionality, not built specifically for prototyping
Marvel	Medium	Good	Easy to learn, fast to build with existing mocks, basic animations	No features for creating elements, limited interactions, hotspots only

NAME OF PROGRAM	FIDELITY	USER TESTING	PROS	CONS
PoP	Low	Medium	Very fast, easy to use, includes some gestures and animations	Limited functionality, must have own mocks or sketches, hotspots only
Principle	High	Good	Timeline-based motion design, good for creating complex interactions and motion quickly	Not optimized for web design, only mobile, cannot view prototypes in a webview, and no Android app
Proto.io	Medium	Average	Can add animations to individual elements, good simulation of complex interactions	Learning curve, difficult to use existing mocks
Solidify	Good	High	Good for click-through prototypes, great for user testing, collects qualitative and quantitative data, some animation options	No animation for individual elements, no features for creating elements in tool
UXPin	Medium	Good	Large library of UI elements, can add animation to individual elements, some import options	Learning curve, limited interactions, no animated transitions or gesture-based interaction

To make a simple clickable prototype from a paper prototype, take a picture of each screen and each additional element that you created to indicate certain interactions. For example, if I'm testing a sign-in screen, I'll have a screen without anything filled out, one that has the forms filled in and an active button, and a transition between clicking the button and the main page (Figure 5-37).

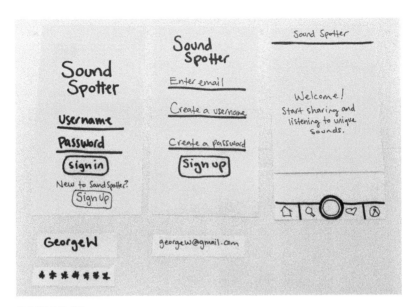

FIGURE 5-37
Example of sign-in paper prototype screens

Upload the individual screens into the software in the order of the user flow, and put hotspots on any interactive areas such as buttons and text fields (Figure 5-38). Then choose what happens when that hotspot is clicked (Figure 5-39). Most often, the only option you have is to link to a different page that you've uploaded or scroll to a different part of the page you're on. Now that you've made a clickable prototype, you can test these prototypes similar to how you did the paper prototypes, but with less work since you won't need to move the paper pieces around during the session.

FIGURE 5-38

The screens being hotspotted together

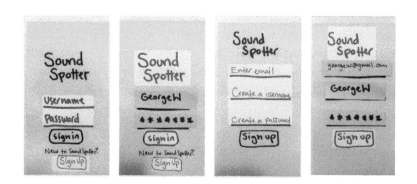

FIGURE 5-39

The final screens with their hotspots

The downside of simple clickable prototypes is that you can't create complex interactions beyond clicking. Some programs allow for general gestures, which helps with mobile-first and app design. Other programs have transitions built in so that you can use animations to add context. Otherwise, you'll need to test that part of your design in a more complex prototyping program. It's not as critical to test animations at the low-fidelity level, but as you progress into mid- and high-fidelity prototypes, you will need more functionality in order to test specific interactions.

Mid-Fidelity Digital Prototypes

Most likely during your prototyping process you'll move fluidly between low-, mid-, and high-fidelity prototypes. You might not even test an idea until you've built it in a mid-fidelity format. Oftentimes, designers will build low-fidelity prototypes to think through the full problem and solution they're solving, and then use a mid-fidelity prototype to test assumptions that they come across during that work.

There are a few different ways that your prototype can be considered mid-fidelity. You can step up the fidelity level in any of the dimensions, so think through which dimension will best support the testing or communication goal you have. If you're early in your process, keep your visual dimension low, and create a prototype with a higher breadth or depth fidelity. That way, you can test how the user navigates through the entire product or accomplishes a specific task, respectively. You can make this level of interaction with clickable prototypes.

If you're later in your process, you can test a prototype with higher visual, interactive, and data model fidelities. Make sure you have real content, and are using the proper terminology for your users. You might need a more interactive medium, so consider building a coded prototype (Figure 5-40), or using a more complex software to create the interactions you need.

FIGURE 5-40

A mid-fidelity coded prototype is in its final medium, and makes it easier to test browser-based interactions

Mix and match the fidelity dimensions based on what you have already designed and what you have access to for content.

MID-FIDELITY CLICKABLE PROTOTYPES

You can make a mid-fidelity prototype by using the same software tools as your low-fidelity clickable prototypes.

Instead of taking pictures of paper wireframes, build out your page designs in a visual software program (like Sketch, Illustrator, or Photoshop) or directly in the prototyping software (like in Axure). Similar to your paper prototypes, draw out each page and interactive element separately.

Usually when you design wireframes, they are static, whole pages. However, when you create the components you need to build a mid-fidelity prototype, you will need to make additional elements and screen duplications. That way, you will have every single interactive pane and element separated out to make it easy to layer and show different responses to user inputs. It's necessary to organize and name your layers and images well so that you can quickly build your prototype with the images. Figures 5-41 and 5-42 illustrate how I keep myself sane in my file structure.

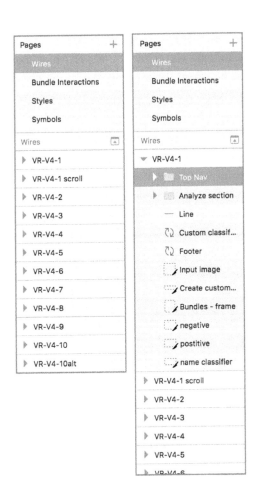

FIGURE 5-41

Name your layers and slices logically so you can know what they are when you export them

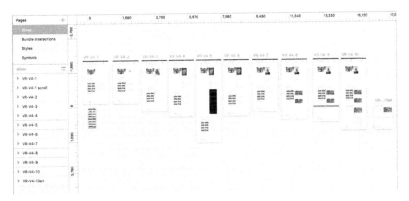

FIGURE 5-42

Organize your artboards so that you can navigate your design files efficiently

If you're using a tool like Sketch or Photoshop, you'll be able to use the Slice tool and layers to save out all the images you need. Otherwise, you'll need to export the elements you've drawn as PNG files. Some prototyping tools allow you to upload the original design file directly, saving you some time and organization when exporting your screens. Check if your prototyping tool has easy import options for Sketch, Photoshop, or Illustrator files.

For example, when testing an image selecting tool, I had to create each "selected image" view (Figure 5-43) so that it would be really easy to show and hide the different panes in the prototyping tool.

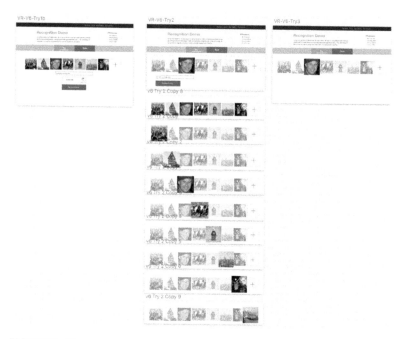

FIGURE 5-43
All of the artboards I created for the different image selections

If this seems rather redundant and tedious, then skip ahead and make a coded prototype instead! If you have the coding skill or are collaborating with a developer, it's much faster to design in-browser for mid- and high-fidelity prototypes. If you can't code or don't have access to developers yet, clickable prototypes are the best way to test your ideas before wasting too much of your developer's time.

You can begin to build higher-fidelity visuals by working with typography, spacing, and colors. This additional context helps your user understand the environment and often directs them to how to accomplish their goals. Make sure to test your visuals during your process instead of relying solely on a grayscale interface.

Think through what order your content will load on the screen and how the panels will move and transition as the user clicks on different buttons and navigation. You can consider using skeletons to indicate what information is coming as it loads, and animate the skeleton to help the user understand their context better. A skeleton consists of subtle boxes that indicate where content will display until it has enough time to load (Figure 5-44).

FIGURE 5-44
Skeletons give your user an idea of what context will load before the content becomes available

Build out your prototype by adding the proper hotspots and choosing the action for each clickable area. Take advantage of any motion capabilities that your prototyping software has, like in Flinto, Principle, or Motion for InVision.

The choices you make for your fidelity will affect which tools you need to use. Refer back to Table 5-1 for details on a variety of current tools. You can make mid-fidelity prototypes in almost any software tool, but specific aspects like motion and complex interactions like drag-and-drop might force you to use a particular one. Choose a tool that you're comfortable with or that you want to learn.

There will always be new tools, so beware of switching up your process too often. Invest your time in learning a shortlist "tool stack" that you can use for all your prototyping purposes instead of learning each new tool as it comes out (Figure 5-45). Like developers who have new frameworks and libraries that come out all the time, keep an eye out for new, better ways to do your work, but don't get distracted or lose too much time learning every single tool.

FIGURE 5-45
Choose your tools wisely, and don't waste too much time learning every new one

Try to test mid-fidelity prototypes on the actual device the product will be used on. This testing will give you vital feedback and allow you to observe how the user uses real inputs such as finger, mouse, or keyboard.

MID-FIDELITY CODED PROTOTYPES

Another way to build a mid-fidelity prototype is to code it. Jumping into code early allows you to test an idea in the actual medium that the final product will be made in. Coding a basic prototype with HTML and CSS is relatively straightforward for mid-fidelity. It allows you to create a responsive design that can be tested across different browsers and devices. Once you get comfortable with code, you might find yourself building out wireframes directly in code to save time. It all depends on the type of digital products you're making and how you prefer to work.

I believe that all designers should at least understand the basics of code and be empowered to create HTML- and CSS-based prototypes. Working with a markup language will help you understand the limitations of your digital medium. Jared Spool, an expert in software usability and research, states "understanding what your medium does well and where isn't as effective makes for more informed design decisions."[3] The better you understand how coded interfaces are built and work, the faster you can design experiences that are implementable and still serve the user.

Coded prototypes should include visual design, even in the initial stages. Visual design should never be left until the end of the process; it should be developed alongside the functionality and fidelity levels of the prototypes. Visual cues help users interact more intuitively with the system, and include spacing, color, typography choices and sizes, and iconography.

It's easy to update and change the visual design of a coded prototype by updating the CSS with styling changes. It's even easier to update and maintain if you use a CSS extension language like Sass (Syntactically Awesome Stylesheets); see Figure 5-46. Sass introduces shortcuts such as variables that you can set at the beginning of your style sheet, like your base colors, and then you can call those variables in the rest of the styles. If your base color changes, you only have to change it in one place to update the color everywhere in your document. To learn more about Sass, check out "The Absolute Beginner's Guide to Sass," which is a great introduction (*http://bit.ly/2gPxKyf*).

---

3 Spool, Jared. "User Interface Engineering," 3 Reasons Why Learning to Code Makes You a Better Designer: UIE Brain Sparks, accessed December 14, 2016. *https://www.uie.com/ brainsparks/2011/06/06/3-reasons-why-learning-to-code-makes-you-a-better-designer/*

CSS	SASS

```
 1  #menu {
 2      margin: 0;
 3      list-style: none;
 4  }
 5
 6  #menu li {
 7      float: left;
 8  }
 9
10  #menu li a {
11      display: block;
12      float: left;
13      padding: 4px 8px;
14      text-decoration: none;
15      background: #2277aa;
16      color: white;
17  }
```

```
 1  $menu_bg: #2277aa
 2
 3  #menu
 4      margin: 0
 5      list-style: none
 6      li
 7          float: left
 8          a
 9              display: block
10              float: left
11              padding: 4px 8px
12              text-decoration: none
13              color: white
14              background: $menu_bg
```

FIGURE 5-46
CSS versus Sass

Coding it yourself

If you're interested in learning how to code your own prototypes, start by downloading a simple text editor and learn basic markup: HTML and CSS. My favorite text editor is Sublime Text (*https://www.sublime-text.com*), and you can download it for free, or optionally pay for it to support the company. There is a multitude of free text editors; choose the one that you prefer, but make sure it has syntax highlighting (where it displays text in specific colors depending on its category of use) as opposed to using a general writing program (Figure 5-47).

FIGURE 5-47

Syntax highlighting in Sublime Text

Some good resources for learning coding and prototyping in code include:

Codeacademy (https://www.codecademy.com)

Free coding courses with side-by-side instruction, code, and display so you can learn and see what you're coding immediately

Bento Front End tracks (https://bento.io/tracks)

Free, full-stack web development training curated from all the best resources online through videos and links to tutorials

Treehouse (https://teamtreehouse.com)

Paid subscription to over 1,000 videos, quizzes, and code challenges

Lynda (https://www.lynda.com)

Paid subscription to extensive library of training videos for not only coding but also design and business

Codepen (http://codepen.io)

Free sandbox environment with side-by-side HTML, CSS, JavaScript, and display panes, and a community with tons of open source code and animations that you can riff off of

There are countless sources of starter code that you can use for coding your layouts. Or you can use any website to kick-start your prototype. In the Google Chrome browser, right-click on a part of a web page and click Inspect, and you can look at the source code and copy it to use in your prototypes (Figure 5-48). It's not ethical to reuse other people's code without permission in production settings, but when you're building prototypes, you can borrow code chunks to make the process faster. You can save your own code snippets for reference to build out quick HTML prototypes too.

FIGURE 5-48

You can use Chrome's Inspect panel to see the source code of any website

Frameworks and pattern libraries that other people have made are a great way to build out ideas faster, including Bootstrap (*http://getbootstrap.com*), AngularJS (*https://angularjs.org*), or Foundation (*http://foundation.zurb.com*). Both types have components that you can put together quickly to build out basic layouts and structures. Frameworks aren't often used for production-level development, but they can help you shortcut your way to building prototypes in browser. Some developers actively avoid using frameworks because they add additional, unused support code and slow down performance speeds. However, your goal is to build quick-and-dirty prototypes to get the best approximation for testing, not to use it as final production code.

The goal of building a coded prototype is to test in the final medium, and to communicate your design intent to the developers and engineers who are building your product. The coded prototype is a rough draft that the developer will rewrite into clean, reusable, bug-less production code, while adding in the backend components that will connect your product to databases, APIs, and additional functionality. They should not be using your code for their final draft.

For example, Figures 5-49 and 5-50 show a basic code outline of a web-app prototype. Feel free to use this code to start your own website prototype!

FIGURE 5-49
This basic coded outline provides a good starting point for coding a website

```
●●●                         ⏚ default.html                    UNREGISTERED

◄ ►      default.html           ✕                                        ▼

1    <!doctype html>
2
3    <html lang="en">
4    <head>
5      <meta charset="utf-8">
6      <title>Website for Testing</title>
7      <meta name="description" content="building this website as a
         coded prototype">
8      <meta name="author" content="Kathryn McElroy">
9      <link rel="stylesheet" href="css/styles.css">
10   </head>
11
12   <body>
13      <header>
14          <h1>Website for Testing</h1>
15          <h2>With basic code that you can use!</h2>
16      </header>
17      <nav>
18          <ul>
19              <li><a href="about.html">about</a></li>
20              <li><a href="contact.html">contact</a></li>
21          </ul>
22      </nav>
23      <section id="Intro">
24          <h3>Hello World!</h3>
25          <p>Here's a paragraph about this product and why it's
             awesome! Here's a paragraph about this product and why
             it's awesome! Here's a paragraph about this product and
             why it's awesome!</p>
26      </section>
27
28      <footer>
29          <p>Copyright 2016 Kathryn McElroy</p>
30          <a href="http://www.youtube.com/">Youtube</a>
31          <a href="http://www.twitter.com/">Twitter</a>
32      </footer>
33
34   </body>
35   </html>

⊟  Line 5, Column 25                          Tab Size: 4          HTML
```

FIGURE 5-50
The code for the previous example

Working with a developer

As you move forward in your prototyping process, it might be best to partner with a frontend developer or engineer to collaborate on building useful prototypes for in-depth testing. As you collaborate closely with a developer to program intricate interactions, you can better understand the feasibility of what you're designing, and test more detailed tasks, including full user flows, purchasing an item, or signing up for a new service. When you need more complex interactions and higher fidelity levels, a developer will use JavaScript, jQuery, or other more powerful programming languages to build them.

To create a coded prototype with a developer, share a well-tested wireframe or clickable prototype to communicate what you need to create. If you're unable to do pair design with your developer, make sure to provide enough context and information about the design and wireframes so that they can code the prototype without much hassle. Ask your developer how they prefer to work, so that you can build a collaborative environment. If you build a good relationship with your developers, your entire team will be able to move faster and work well together.

Work with your developer to scope the functionality of the prototype. If you're only testing a specific part of the app or software, you don't need every link and button to be actively coded. Make sure they know what has to be clickable. It's helpful to include your written or drawn-out user flow for the specific prototype so that your developer understands the goal and functionality of the prototype.

Specify up front the devices you're going to be testing the prototype on. If you're building a smartphone app, you only need to test at a small-screen size. If you're building a web app, you will want a responsive prototype that can be tested at multiple screen sizes. Finally, if you're doing remote user testing, you'll need to host your code online so that they can access the prototype.

It might seem overwhelming to make coded prototypes. However, like any skill, the more you work on it and learn new aspects of code, the better you'll get at communicating with your developers and understanding your medium. Being able to code your own prototypes is a valuable job skill that can land you new positions in the future. It pays to be able to build and test your ideas in a more authentic way.

High-Fidelity Digital Prototypes

Now that you've worked out most of your assumptions through prototyping and user testing, and fixed any big problems along the way, you can create high-fidelity prototypes to bring all of your learning and design together.

The best approach to testing at this level is to create a high-fidelity coded prototype. Work with a developer to make a functional, coded version of your final product. If you don't have the coding capability or access to developers to help, then you'll need to fake it by creating high-fidelity clickable prototypes. The best way to do this is to use a visual design program like Illustrator or Sketch to lay out exactly how the product will look and a prototyping tool like InVision, Flinto, or Axure to add interactions and detailed animations.

The specific tool doesn't matter as much as the execution of prototype. It should include the end-to-end experience of your product (both breadth and depth), high-fidelity visual design (this is the time for pixel-perfect), real user data and content (both images and written material), any motion or animations, and interactions. It's still a prototype, so the entire system and the backend might not be present, but the parts that are should look exactly like the expected, final product (Figure 5-51).

FIGURE 5-51
High-fidelity prototypes are much more polished

At this point in your process, you're testing minute details and interactions. Is the font size appropriate for the different media sizes? Are the animations adding to the experience and not distracting the user? Is the content easy to read, and are the calls to action clear and accessible? You can conduct longer, more detailed tests, and users can tackle complex tasks.

When you test a high-fidelity prototype, you should look for any problems that the user has with the experience. That includes clarity of wording in UI text and calls to action, navigation, task flow, and understanding where they are in the system. These aspects might seem like broader concepts, but if your user has these problems with a high-fidelity prototype, you might need to re-create the interactions at a mid-fidelity to better test that part. Depending on your prototyping goal, you can flow back and forth between mid- and high-fidelity work in order to best test and communicate the different parts of the product.

Just like for mid-fidelity, you'll need to organize and keep track of your files well to save time and your sanity (Figure 5-52). In your visual design software, take the time to properly arrange and name your artboards. By taking five minutes to organize your files, you'll save tons of time when you export all the images out to build your prototype in the prototyping software. You'll also help your colleagues if they need to reference your files or take over the project in the future. I try to organize my artboard based on user flow, with alternatives arranged below the primary idea, and name them based on the use of the exported image.

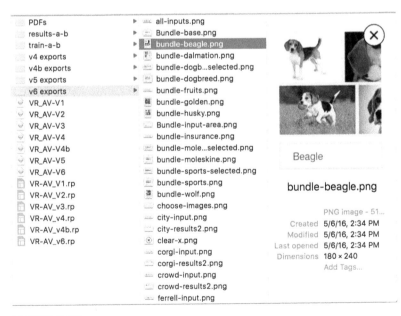

FIGURE 5-52

File organization of Sketch exports in a Finder window

You can change your mid-fidelity files to high fidelity by updating the symbols you created with better and more accurate visual design. You can also use the Shared Styles and Text Styles (in Sketch) or Graphic Styles and Character Styles (in Illustrator) to quickly update the colors and text attributions across your design. Taking advantage of these shortcut tools will help you be more efficient.

Use plugins, like Zeplin for Sketch, to seamlessly translate your designs to redlines and style guides for your developers (Figure 5-53). Keep an eye out for new tools that help speed up communication between you and your teammates.

FIGURE 5-53
Zeplin specs out all of your designs to make it easier to communicate to developers

HIGH-FIDELITY CLICKABLE PROTOTYPES

High-fidelity clickable prototypes are a good way to build out a fully designed interface without code (Figure 5-54). These clickable prototypes take more skill and time due to the execution of the visual design and the interactions you create in the prototyping sofware. For example, if you need to test a drag-and-drop area, it's very difficult to re-create that in a hotspot-based prototyping software. You'll need to use a more powerful, and complex, software like Axure, which has a higher learning curve and takes longer to use. Make sure to take into account which tool you need to use so that you can properly plan your work and time commitment.

FIGURE 5-54
A high-fidelity clickable prototype should be almost indistinguishable from the real, final product, even though it's not coded

Feasibility

When you're building non-coded, high-fidelity prototypes, you need to understand exactly what's possible to deliver. Since you're not building your interface in its final medium, it's possible that you'll create motions and interactions that aren't possible to code. Get feedback on your prototypes from developers who know how the work will need to be implemented and programmed. They'll be able to estimate how long it takes to code different aspects of the design. Make sure you understand the feasibility for motion and animations and their effects on the performance of the product.

Performance means the speed that the page loads when a user lands on it. Every image you add and line of code that's required to build your design adds time to the loading of a page and makes your user wait longer (Figure 5-55). You must balance the visual and content requirements of your design with its performance to enable the best experience for your user. For more information on performance, read Lara Hogan's book *Designing for Performance* (O'Reilly).

FIGURE 5-55

Your design has a direct impact on the performance and load times of the pages

When showing a high-fidelity prototype to your business stakeholders, know your feasibility and performance limitations. When you present your high-fidelity work, try to underpromise so that you can overdeliver. If you're unsure if your developers have the time to implement a specific animation, display an alternative that you know can be built. Then later, if your developer has the time to do the more complex animation, it's an added bonus instead of a letdown if they can't deliver.

Frame your high-fidelity work properly because your business stakeholders will assume that what they see is exactly what they'll get. Explain to them that it's a visual mock-up instead of implemented code, so that they have a better understanding of how the product is translated from visuals to clean code. Be reasonable with what you know the development team can accomplish and set your stakeholders' expectations well.

Content

Your high-fidelity prototype should have all of the final content and the proper data models in place (Figure 5-56). At this point, you should not have any lorem ipsum (placeholder text) in your layouts and designs. You should add content to your interface to best reflect the exact terminology and user data that will appear in your product. One way to keep track of your content is to have it saved in a Word document or spreadsheet. As your business stakeholders and information developers update the content, your source should update too so that you can incorporate it into the prototype.

FIGURE 5-56

High-fidelity prototypes should have real content

It can be easier to add content with plug-ins for certain prototyping software. The Craft plug-in from InVision Labs allows you to dynamically add real content to your screen layouts in Sketch (Figure 5-57). As more design companies and tech firms realize the benefit of designing with real user data and information, more tools will help make it faster and easier to do such. Check if there are already new tools that will help you in your current workflow.

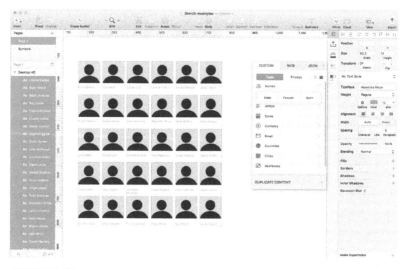

FIGURE 5-57
The Craft plug-in for Sketch has a Data feature that populates real data for your high-fidelity designs, such as the names shown here

A/B Testing

Once you have your high-fidelity prototype made, you can conduct additional A/B tests to make refinements. When you conduct an A/B test, you compare two versions of the same interface with slight variations to see which one is easier for the user to navigate or use.

Choose which aspects of the design need to be A/B tested. They can be small details, like the text on a call to action, or they can be completely different layouts for the page. The best way to determine what can be A/B tested is whenever you have multiple ways you can do something, and you're unsure which way makes more sense to a user. Instead of blindly choosing the version that your gut tells you, you can test both versions and let the user decide.

Create a prototype for both versions of the interface, and set up your user test so that the same task can be completed in each version. In the user test, have the user complete the task in both interfaces back to back. Observe any issues that they have with the user flow. You may ask the user which one was easier or more intuitive to use for the task. Combine your observations and their perspective to guide your choice. As you conduct this test multiple times, switch the order of the interfaces in the test so that you don't bias the results because the user already knows how to complete the task.

Business stakeholders appreciate A/B tests because it gives them empirical data to support the direction you choose instead of only trying one way of designing the interface. Wield your A/B tests well, and determine which tests would benefit most from the added time that it takes to build a second prototype interface.

HIGH-FIDELITY CODED PROTOTYPES

The IBM Mobile Innovation Lab (MIL) regularly builds high-fidelity prototypes of app ideas, and then releases coded versions to the open source community, in order to share and build on different IBM technologies' capabilities. For example, a team of designers and developer created a travel experience app for business and groups of travelers, to aid in booking and planning trips and vacations.

After mapping the user flow through the entire experience, the team chose to prototype the happy path to test the main functionality. The designers, Sushi Sutasirisap and Alana Louise, with research help from Becca Shuman & Aide Gutierrez-Gonzalez, created a mid-fidelity clickable prototype using Sketch and InVision (Figure 5-58). They got feedback that some of the pop-ups didn't make sense to the user, so they changed that aspect of the design before making the next round of prototype.

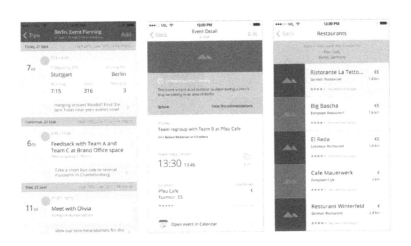

FIGURE 5-58
A mid-fidelity version of the MIL Travel App

The designers then combined their work with the developers, who were simultaneously making a backend to the experience, to build out a high-fidelity prototype using Swift and Xcode (Figure 5-59). The goal was to communicate the functionality and scope of the app, so they created very specific user flows within the prototype to show their users' happy paths. Within the prototype, they built in a "God Mode" that allowed the testing facilitator to trigger specific events, like a change in weather or the user selecting a transportation option (Figure 5-60). By using specific triggers, they could test the user's reaction to real-world situations without relying on the weather to cooperate.

The backend of the app doesn't work 100%, and they had to fake a little bit of the data, but the demo is connected to the proper databases and backend to allow a non-IBM developer to take this code as a starting place, and plug it into their own application. The code for their Swift prototype is open source and available to build off of at GitHub (*http://bit.ly/2hfVWvJ*).

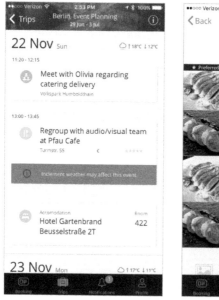

FIGURE 5-59

The high-fidelity MIL Travel App coded with Swift and Xcode

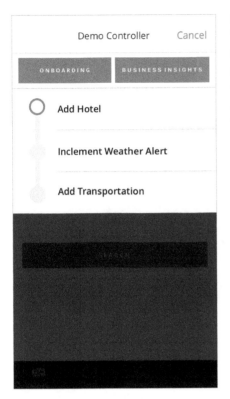

FIGURE 5-60

The designers added a "God Mode" to be able to trigger specific weather alerts, such as heavy rain or bad traffic

They Got It Right—IBM MIL

The MIL also took on a large project to redefine and improve wayfinding and amenities usage in large venues such as museums, theme parks, and stadiums (Figure 5-61). The team, made up of developers, designers, and user researchers, explored how to increase engagement and improve the quality of the venues' amenities, such as concessions, signage, souvenir shops, and social media interactions.

By conducting interviews and visiting Six Flags and the Dallas Cowboys Stadium (now AT&T Stadium), the team discovered a couple specific users that they would need to address in different ways. Their solution would need to help visitors to the venue engage and get around, and it would need to help venue owners get feedback and understand their visitors in order to improve their venues over time.

FIGURE 5-61

The team initially researched theme parks to develop their immersive experience (image courtesy of Flickr user David Fulmer)

More specifically, visitors have a set of needs, including finding a specific work of art, attraction, or their seat; getting information about a collection, roller coaster, or game details; and having that information be contextual and tailored for their specific use. Venue owners have their own set of goals, including understanding and tracking visitor behavior overall, seeing which amenities or collections were most or least visited, and tracking how promotions are being used or not used by the visitors.

As the designers and user researchers dug into the personas and research, the development team explored a variety of technologies that might contribute to the solution. They especially looked at *beacons*, small Bluetooth-based sensors that send contextual information or directions to smartphones when they are in proximity to the sensor (Figure 5-62). They also considered a multimodal approach that allows for multiple touch points throughout the venue.

FIGURE 5-62
They considered using Bluetooth beacons for contextual information and directions (image courtesy of Flickr user Jona Nalder)

The designers and developers came together to prototype and test their ideas in a few different levels and locations. First they did exploratory solutioning for wayfinding at a museum. They observed how visitors interacted with existing wayfinding at the museum. Then, back at their office, they created a paper prototype of alternative signage for a generalized use case and conducted tests to determine if a user could find their way better (Figure 5-63). They used statements like "where would you go to accomplish" a specific task, then let the user walk through the office, taking note of which signs they looked at and how long it took them to navigate to specific areas.

From this user test, they discovered just how little time signage has to make an impact on a visitor. Participants would glance at signage for less than three seconds before making a snap judgement on where to go next. The design team took that insight, and did additional research and work around iconography to enable quick glances to be enough to properly direct visitors.

FIGURE 5-63
The user research team created paper prototypes of the wayfinding system

Next, the team tested digital prototypes of the visitor application, first focusing on the context of theme parks. They chose to scope the design to one type of interaction and venue in order to best test the assumptions around the interaction patterns. They also wanted to find out what information was a top priority for the user. They assumed that ride details, offers, and gamification badges would be top priority. They built the smartphone app prototype with Illustrator and InVision, and tested which parts were most helpful to users based on the specific scenario (Figure 5-64).

The testing insights revealed that people weren't concerned about badges as the main focus goal of their theme park visit. The users really liked the idea of badges or offers only if it was something that automatically happened in the background as the day went by and as they explored the theme park. They also learned that besides ride details, people were mostly interested in successfully keeping in touch with the rest of their group during their visit, as well as real-time updates on rides' availability when inclement weather conditions existed.

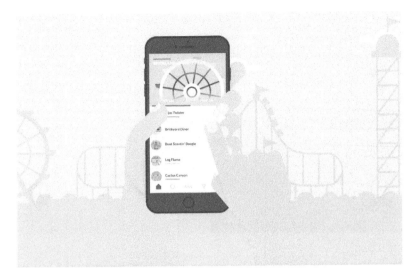

FIGURE 5-64
Mid-fidelity InVision prototype design, as shown in promotion video

After this round of testing, the project pivoted to focus on a stadium application because it was a better target market for the multimodal approach, and the team had connections with users in order to test their more robust prototypes. They spent six weeks building out a full system prototype that included not only the visitor smartphone app, but also the venue owner's interface and additional smart screens and experiences.

The whole team, both designers and developers, collaborated to make the high-fidelity prototype experience. The developers built a unified database to connect the iPhone app for visitors and an iPad dashboard for venue owners. Both applications were coded in Swift, based on the updated designs and testing. They also built a tvOS (Apple's television operating system) app to create their smart screens that would react based on iPhone proximity (Figure 5-65).

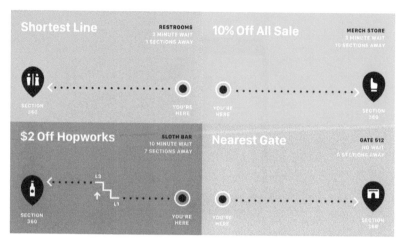

FIGURE 5-65

The team created prototypes of the stadium smart screens on tvOS

The iPhone app allows visitors to easily find their personal stadium seat and navigate around the concourse to different amenities, get real-time information and alerts about the game, get promotions based on their stadium interactions, and challenge their friends to gain points and badges throughout the game (Figure 5-66). This part of the prototype was created with Swift using MVVM and Reactive Cocoa (an open source library that brings Reactive Programming to the Objective-C language) to propagate events and data as fast as possible to the user. They used real data from a previously played football game to give the full context of the experience to the user.

The iPad dashboard allows venue owners to track analytics and insights from all of that customer information, so that they can improve their venue and ensure visitor engagement (Figure 5-67). Alerts and real-time data tracking enables the owner to better crowd-form to alleviate congestion and drive sales in certain parts of the stadium. From the interface, they can also send promotions to targeted visitors during the game to increases sales and engagement. The designers built this prototype with Flinto to simulate the animations and interactions of the dashboard. This prototype uses simulated data based on estimated analytics from their initial stadium research.

FIGURE 5-66

The final iPhone app delivered a seamless experience no matter where the user interacted with it

FIGURE 5-67

The final iPad app for venue owners receives real-time data from visitors and analytics from the venue's amenities

The team's final prototyped experience had two main physical areas that the user interacted with: first they entered the "concourse area" with smart screens for contextual information and wayfinding, and then they found their seat in the "stadium" with the game simulation playing on a screen and Megatron showing additional promotions and information (see Figures 5-68 and 5-69).

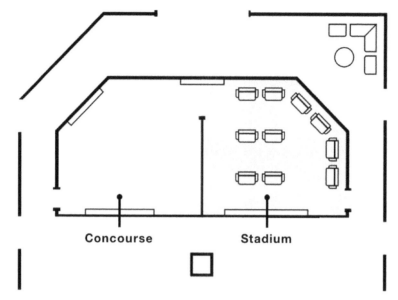

Concourse   **Stadium**

FIGURE 5-68

The team created an experience center where users could actually walk through and interact with the different parts of the multimodal experience

FIGURE 5-69

The final experience was immersive and detailed

The MIL team not only used this prototyped environment to test the experience with users; they also used it as a communication tool to show executives and potential stadium clients how this project could bring value to their venue. This project inspired the team to keep exploring other solutions that combine multiple technologies, by helping them realize how well received a cohesive and detailed experience was.

Overall, this six-month project evolved and shifted based on the team's research and prototypes. In the end, they were able to make a complex, multimodal digital experience come to life with a little creativity and spatial planning. For each step of the process, they decided on a scope for their prototype, careful not to take on too much to build and test within each iteration. By working on smaller parts of the interactions, they were able to improve them individually before combining them into the larger, full experience.

Summary

Digital products have similar and different prototyping needs than physical products. Your medium for software and apps is code, and your interaction method is screens. When designing for screens, you have the opportunity to use motion and animation to guide your users through their experience. Animation must be used judiciously, but when it's applied well, it makes a product enjoyable to use and easy to navigate.

Other unique aspects include designing responsive and mobile-first, if you're creating a web app that can be viewed on many different devices. If you design from a mobile-first point of view, it will be easier and faster to make that design translate into larger screens. Different types of interaction and accessibility are other valuable features to test and try out. Your users might be using touch, voice, or keyboard and mouse to interact with your product. Decide which interactions make sense for your specific user, then ensure you're testing those specific types of interaction in your prototypes.

Finally, accessibility is crucial so that you create a universally open web with the products you ship. Consider how people of all ability levels will use your product, and include all types of people in your user testing. Your color might not have a high enough contrast ratio for low-visibility or color-blind users. You might not be able to use only a keyboard to navigate through the product. Both of these aspects are necessary for certain segments of people who will need to use your product, so consider their needs during your development and prototyping work.

Prepare yourself for success by creating a user flow for your product and one for your specific prototype. Riff off this flow by sketching many different ways to create the interactions your user needs to complete the flow. These sketches might be on Post-its and paper, and later in the visual design program of your choice. This is the time to work on the information architecture of your site or product.

As you establish a direction you'd like to pursue, you can make low-fidelity prototypes, including wireframes, paper prototypes, and clickable prototypes. Choose what assumption you need to test, then determine which part of the user flow you need in the prototype in order to test that assumption. It's a similar process for mid-fidelity prototypes, but with more resolution around content, visuals, or the other dimensions of fidelity. You can make coded prototypes on your own or by partnering with developers to get enough functionality to test in the final medium of the browser.

At a high-fidelity level, you can test more detailed aspects of your product. It's good to test your animations at this level to ensure that they're providing enough value to be worth the development effort. You can get a better understanding of the feasibility and time to develop your design by using high-fidelity prototypes to communicate with your development team.

Use these prototyping types and fidelity levels as a toolkit from which you can pull what you need, when you need to. Remember to write out the assumptions you're testing, and then choose the proper fidelity level and type of prototype you need to prove or disprove that assumption. The best user experience designers and prototypers don't depend on one tool; they have a whole arsenal of options that they're comfortable with, and choose which one to use for each specific engagement.

You now have the tools you need to take an app or software idea from your head and make it into a tested, polished product.

[6]

Prototyping for Physical Products

PERSONAL ELECTRONICS AND PHYSICAL computing are booming areas of design right now. The price of electrical components has dropped, making them more accessible to design and create products with embedded sensors. It's easy to connect these devices with other Internet of Things (IoT) objects throughout the home or office. These products often have both a physical component and a software app that controls or interacts with the functions of the device. The main focus of this chapter is smart objects, wearables, and connected IoT products. I won't be digging into traditional industrial design and form-making, which has its own rigorous prototyping practices. In this chapter, I'll set you up for success while giving you the real lowdown on hurdles you'll need to overcome to create useful prototypes for physical products.

Getting Started with Electronics

There are so many ways to get started and involved in electronics. New kits come out often that help you build custom circuits and systems including kits from littleBits (*littlebits.cc*), Adafruit (*www.adafruit.com*), and SparkFun (*www.sparkfun.com*). Some kits contain a micro-controller (the computer chip brain), breadboard (solderless construction base), connectors, and a variety of sensors and outputs. These kits, such as the one shown in Figure 6-1, are a great way to get started building simple circuits.

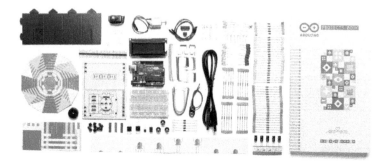

FIGURE 6-1

An Arduino starter kit is a great way to get all the materials you need (*https:// www.arduino.cc/en/Main/ArduinoStarterKit*)

You can purchase specific themed kits with motors (*www.adafruit.com/ products/171*), **WiFi** (*www.adafruit.com/products/2680*) and Bluetooth connections (*www.adafruit.com/products/3026*), sensors (e.g., heat, motion, touch, etc., at *www.adafruit.com/products/176*), and lights (including RGB LEDs that can change color or LEDs in all shades of the rainbow here *www.sparkfun.com/products/12903*). Other kits, such as the one shown in Figure 6-2, have all the components necessary to build a specific device—in this case, a robot. Each of these is a fun way to try out electronics with a low investment and lower learning curve.

You can build with individual components and sensors that allow you to combine the exact inputs and outputs that will address your specific need. After a lot of work and testing, you can partner with industrial designers and engineers to build out the proper schematic and specs, work with a manufacturer, and scale your design to a production level to be sold as a product.

It's simple to create a new idea for the Internet of Things, but by making a prototype (such as the one shown in Figure 6-3), testing your concept, and pitching a working version of your idea, you'll be much more likely to get a business stakeholder to buy in and invest. You'll be taken more seriously, and you'll be able to clearly demonstrate the benefit of your new product.

FIGURE 6-2

This kit (*www.adafruit.com/products/749*) helps you build a robot that can use antennae to change direction when it hits something

FIGURE 6-3

A physical prototype can help take your idea out of your head and communicate it to others

It's common to encounter roadblocks along the development process with new electronic devices. The field is crowded, and you need a clear value proposition for your idea, or the main reason why a user will choose your product over others. Keep the problem you're solving at the front of your mind during the prototyping process. By maintaining a user-centered approach, you will set yourself apart from the majority of the hobbyist crowd, and create a successful electronic device.

What's Unique for Physical Products

Prototyping for physical products has a few essential features and processes that are not the same as digital products. The main aspects you must take into account are the electronics and coding involved in its functionality and the materials and tactility of the physical product.

ELECTRONICS

It may seem overwhelming to begin working with electronics, but it's such a fun and engaging way to prototype! You will get your hands dirty building out physical representations of your product idea, and that's part of the fun. You can test your idea and communicate it to improve it. The benefit of designing a smart object or wearable device is that you get to choose exactly the parts that make it work. You don't have to be dependent on a smartphone manufacturer or specific operating system; you can invent how you want the product to function.

The downside of designing your physical product is that you'll need to purchase and understand how to use the electronic components to make your prototypes. These components include how you collect information with sensors, including temperature, light, sound, motion, and pressure sensors or analog dials (Figure 6-4). You need to decide how the device will interact with a network or other devices such as a phone or computer (Bluetooth, WiFi, or cord). Finally, you'll design the different outputs such as lights, sound, visualizations, or haptics.

You can start by working with starter kits to build familiarity with the variety of components that are available. One example is littleBits, which has magnetic components that snap together to build simple circuits with inputs and outputs (Figure 6-5). Although it's primarily designed for kids, this style of kit helps you get started, and allows you to create very low-fidelity prototypes as well as invent fun use cases for the different components. It makes it simple to build ideas without needing very much electronics knowledge. It doesn't require soldering, so its learning curve is low.

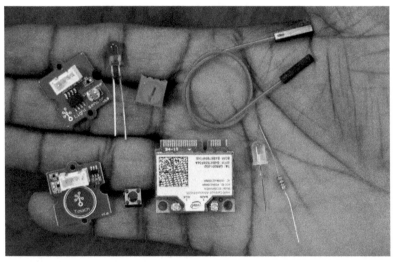

FIGURE 6-4

You'll need a variety of components to make your electrical prototypes (photo courtesy of Flickr user Intel Free Press)

FIGURE 6-5

A littleBits kit comes with many components that snap together using magnets (*http://littlebits.cc/kits/rule-your-room-kit*)

As you progress, you can purchase other more intricate kits that support your idea, such as the motor kit from Adafruit shown in Figure 6-6. After a while, you'll build up a collection of spare parts, and you'll be surprised how quickly you'll be able to prototype ideas using the materials around you.

FIGURE 6-6

This motor kit from Adafruit has many different types of motors to build with (*https://www.adafruit.com/products/1438*)

Once you get more comfortable with simple circuits, you can start building more complex circuits with microcontrollers. A microcontroller is a computer chip that acts as the brain for your electronic prototype (Figure 6-7). You can write code for the microcontroller in order to control what it does. Most microcontrollers can take input from sensors, analyze it based on the code you've written, and push out the proper response to the user. Or it can send that information to the smartphone app for it to display that information to the user, like an activity tracker does.

As you want more control over the inner-workings of your physical prototype, you'll need to work with custom code and raw components rather than kits. When you start building higher-fidelity prototypes, you'll most likely need to solder your components together. Soldering isn't very difficult, but it does require equipment (Figure 6-8), and it takes a bit of practice to get the hang of it.

FIGURE 6-7
An Arduino Uno microcontroller provides the brains of your electronic prototype

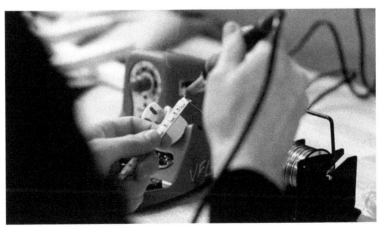

FIGURE 6-8
An entry-level soldering iron

CODING AND TROUBLESHOOTING

The code you write and use for electronic prototypes is different than coded prototypes for digital products. This type of code is in a different language, and actually controls all of the components that are attached to the microcontroller. You can equate it with the backend coding of a web app, but there's more to the functionality within the microcontroller's loop and variables. You'll need to write code, but there are shortcuts that will help you get going faster.

By taking part in the open source community (where people share their code and projects online for others to build upon), you can get a head start on your code, and share back with the community when you're done. There's so much support for sharing code online that it shouldn't be difficult to get at least a general understanding of how to write the specific code you need.

Along with code comes the indisputable need for troubleshooting. Code can be very temperamental, and you must use very specific commands and structure to get it to work. If you have a missing comma, or an additional bracket, your microcontroller might not be able to see your sensor or process the math you're asking it to. This fact is why I recommend testing in smaller units before combining all of your components together immediately. Start by writing the code for each individual component and testing them. The more components and code you have in one prototype, the more likely there will be a bug, and the harder it will be to find which individual piece of code or circuit connection is causing the problem.

Later on, I'll give you tips on how to troubleshoot when you eventually need to. (Everybody does!) It can be frustrating, but you'll feel the most pure moment of joy when you figure out what's wrong with your code or circuit and fix it, and your prototype works perfectly.

MATERIALS AND TACTILITY

Materials are a significant part of physical products; it's an added dimension of the product experience. You control how the surface feels, and how the various outputs interact with the user's sense of touch. This tactile interaction is part of stand-alone smart objects, but even more so for wearable technology that is in constant contact with the user. Different materials are better or worse for this application (Figure 6-9). As you're designing the functionality in the electronics, you need to decide where the product will reside, either within the house (shelf, countertop, bedside) or on the body (wrist, neck, upper arm), and how it will interact (light, sound, vibration motors).

FIGURE 6-9
Wearable technology needs different materials depending on its application (image courtesy of Flickr user Intel Free Press)

Create a user flow for your device idea to help you understand how the materials will affect the user. Where will the user mainly interact with it? Decide if this device will stay in one place or be taken with the user wherever they go. Does the user touch this product once a day or once a month? All of these factors will help you to decide on the type of materials that are necessary, so include them in the user flow of the product.

When designing for non-wearable smart objects, keep in mind the environment in which those objects will live. How can you best prototype and test your idea in its real environment? If you're designing a smart bathroom scale, you'd want to try it out on all possible bathroom floor types, and in all sizes of bathroom. A scale that works in an expansive bathroom with tile might not work in a tiny studio apartment bathroom with carpet. And the material of the housing will need to work for tile, linoleum, or carpeted floors.

Useful considerations for wearables are ensuring materials won't cause allergic reactions, and thinking through how the object will need to be maintained or cleaned. For example, if you're designing a sports-related wearable, consider silicon or neoprene as materials that can stand up to sweat and constant motion. Or if your wearable is designed as a jewelry piece, decide on a metal finish that doesn't cause skin irritation, and avoid metals such as nickel that commonly cause allergic reactions. You might consider putting the electronics in a housing that can be removed and cleaned, like Fitbit or Misfit does with their activity tracker bands (Figure 6-10). The band that touches the skin is cleanable, and you can take the small electronic component out of the band in order to clean it.

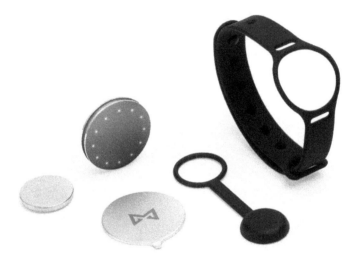

FIGURE 6-10
The band for Misfit detaches from the electronics to allow for easy cleaning

Throughout your process, you can use prototyping to test different types of materials, forms, and placements to help you decide which direction to go (Figure 6-11). Once you decide where the object will reside, try to test your prototypes as close as possible to the final position on the body and with the proper materials, so that you can get feedback on the form and material concerns. You might find with testing that the wrist isn't the best place for your device (especially with all the other devices that currently reside there) and configure an alternative band that allows the user to place your product on their upper arm or ankle.

FIGURE 6-11
Material selection is crucial for prototypes of physical products

You'll be choosing a few different types of materials for your product. The surface and finishing materials are what the user interacts with, such as plastics, wood veneers, or fabrics. Another material type you'll need to consider is the build material that will be used to manufacture your product (such as injection-molded plastic, or CNC-milled aluminum). For more information about material design, check out these books:

- *Materials for Design* by Chris Lefteri (Laurence King Publishing)

- *Making It: Manufacturing Techniques for Product Design* by Chris Lefteri (Laurence King Publishing)

- *Materials and Design* by Mike Ashby and Kara Johnson (Butterworth-Heinemann)

The material choice contributes to the tactility of the product. What are the literal touch points that your product needs? You might need a screen, buttons, haptics, or motion sensors to pick up specific user gestures (Figure 6-12). The decisions you make about the tactile components will help you decide on what prototypes you need to build to test these components, separately and then together as a product.

FIGURE 6-12
Physical prototypes need specific touch points

Each component has a variety of different types and shapes that you can purchase. For a button, how do you want the click to feel: mechanical with a noise, or smooth and seamless? You should order a few different types of buttons to try out on different prototypes, like an arcade button versus a smaller smooth button (Figure 6-13). Screen size can affect the tactility of the surface by forming the entire clickable area. Choose the right size of screen for the size of your interface. You might have tactile controls such as a dial or slider. As the designer, you get to choose what those interactions feel like and how they contribute to the overall experience and personality of your product, whereas with digital products you only get to choose how the interface looks instead of how it feels to the touch.

FIGURE 6-13
A variety of buttons—
"Tactility includes
the interactive points
of your product, like
buttons, screens, and
anything that touches
the user"

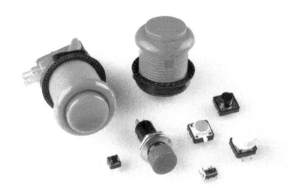

Preparation

Before you begin prototyping, take time to prepare your idea and prototype plan so that you know exactly what you need to create. Based on the prototyping process you're following (see Chapter 4), you should already have an understanding of who your users are and the problem that you're solving for them. You might have written out your user flow to understand your user's interaction points or written out an assumption if you're going to use the prototype to test it.

Use these assets to determine the scope of the prototype you're making (one component, multiple, or the whole experience) and what functionality you'll need to code into the prototype. This is a good time to revisit the different dimensions of fidelity in Chapter 3, to prioritize the dimensions for this prototype's use.

For example, if I'm building a wearable activity tracker and want to test how it fits into the user's daily life and the comfort of the device, I need a higher fidelity of breadth to get an overview of the user's interactions (Figure 6-14). However, I don't need to go as deep into the individual activities that the band can track because I'm focusing on the top level of the interactions. For this prototype, I would focus on the materials and basic inputs (buttons) and outputs (lights and vibration) to indicate what would happen tracking-wise, but without actually implementing the data tracking or connecting it with a smartphone app for consuming tracking metrics.

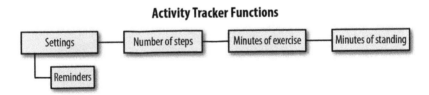

Activity Tracker Functions

FIGURE 6-14
In this diagram, I show the breadth and depth of the prototype I need to build for an activity tracker

In addition to a user flow and scoping based on the assumption you're testing, it is helpful to create an initial circuit diagram and to purchase the components you need. These two points are a bit of a chicken-and-egg problem, and can always be updated. You can do either one first, but it may be helpful to understand how your components will tie together before purchasing them.

If you're new to electronics, this is a great time to read up on some of the basics of how electronics work, so that you understand what materials you'll need and basic safety. My favorite resources for foundational understanding include this Basic Electronics Instructable (*http://www.instructables.com/id/Basic-Electronics/?ALLSTEPS*) and this learning series from SparkFun (*learn.sparkfun.com/tutorials/where-do-i-start#starter-tutorials*). The safety concerns are real when you're working with electricity, so be safe and make sure you understand enough to not get shocked or set your prototype on fire!

CIRCUIT DIAGRAMS

Circuit diagrams or sketches are a good first step in designing the functionality of your smart object prototype. Based on your user flow and scope, decide which components will be part of your prototype. This sketch will determine how the different components interact with each other and the microcontroller that controls everything (Figure 6-15). Either draw on paper, or plug together on a microcontroller and breadboard, your basic circuit for how the different pieces will connect together (Figure 6-16). These low-fidelity sketches are your first step to making a *schematic*, a detailed diagram showing all the electrical components in a circuit in order to have it professionally manufactured as a circuit board.

FIGURE 6-15

You can draw a circuit to think through how the pieces should go together

FIGURE 6-16
Or you can make a breadboard circuit to try out simple circuits

You can build your circuits digitally in programs like Fritzing (*fritzing. org/home*), an open source hardware initiative that has libraries of components to build intricate circuits. Once you've laid out your circuit in Fritzing, you can view it as a schematic or a printed circuit board (PCB) to check how it will look and function.

Or if you haven't made circuits before, write out in a story how the different sensors and outputs will work together and draw how they interact. You can use a standard "if this then that" approach to write the story. For example, for a remote smart sensor for dogs:

- If the motion sensor is activated by a dog
- Then take a picture
- Then text that picture to the owner's phone number
- If the motions sensor is not activated, do nothing

Based on this story, I know that I need a motion sensor input, a camera input, a microcontroller that is connected to WiFi, and a backend that will text the image to a phone number. Figure 6-17 shows a quick representation of this story in a circuit.

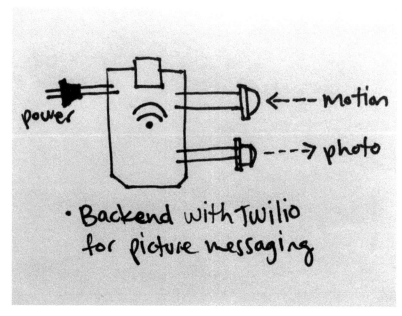

FIGURE 6-17
Illustration of this circuit in a diagram

That story gives me a good jumping-off point so that I can purchase the proper components I need, and it gives me a head start on my pseudo-code so that I can write the code I need for my microcontroller.

Circuit diagrams and breadboard circuits are both prototypes to test with your electrically minded friends. Show them your diagram and have them tell you what they think this circuit does. If they get it right, great! If not, you can share how your prototype should work and get her or his feedback on how to improve your circuit diagram.

OBTAINING MATERIALS

The next step in preparation is to purchase the components and materials you need to build your prototype. Electronics and components range in price from pennies per resistor to hundreds of dollars for LED arrays (Figure 6-18). You need to get the specific components for your prototype, but there are ways to prototype interactive ideas without purchasing the most expensive version of the component. You can build analogous tests that indicate an interaction, but use a different component than the final to test it. Or you can code an HTML version of your idea, such as an LED array that can be very expensive, and test it with users before investing in the actual component itself.

FIGURE 6-18
Cheap versus expensive
components

You might want to set up your electronics workspace with some basic materials including wire, wire cutters, a soldering iron and solder, a multimeter, a variety of LEDs, a breadboard, a multipack of resistors, some buttons, knobs, and dials, and a few different sensors (Figure 6-19). By purchasing this short list of components, you'll have what you need to build a good portion of your initial low-fidelity prototypes. At some point, you'll need microcontrollers, and there are many to choose from.

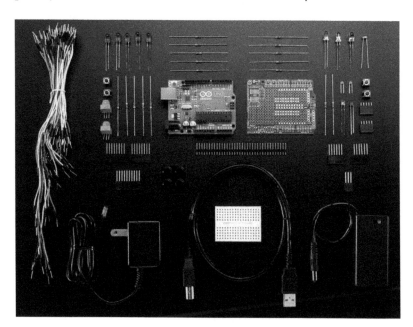

FIGURE 6-19
Purchasing a starter pack of components is a great way to start building many prototypes (*http://www.adafruit.com/products/68*)

Some of my favorite microcontrollers to have on hand include the Arduino Uno, Arduino Micro, Trinket, Gemma and Flora (for sewing), and Photon (for WiFi). They range in price from $7–$25 and have different capabilities (Table 6-1). Some of the less expensive microcontrollers don't have serial input (taking information in from the cord), but they are really good for cheap prototypes. Another factor for choosing which microcontroller to use for your prototype is its size. Low-fidelity prototypes can use larger microcontrollers, like the Uno, but you'll need to move to smaller ones as your designs get more refined. At the end of your prototyping process, you'll most likely design your own circuit board and microcontroller to fit your exact specifications, but until then, you should be fine testing with existing ones.

TABLE 6-1. Some of the best microcontrollers, with specifics on price, what they're good for, and how many available pins they have

NAME	PRICE	BEST FOR	# OF ANALOG AND DIGITAL PINS	LANGUAGE
Arduino Uno	$24.95	Great introductory level, easy to use, especially with a breadboard	6, 14	Arduino/C variant
Arduino Mega	$45.95	Huge and powerful, has more memory and pins	16, 54	Arduino/C variant
Raspberry Pi	$39.95	Linux computer in a board, HDMI outputs and video HD capable video processor	None (no onboard ADC), 8	Any language supported by a compatible Linux distribution
Trinket	$6.95	Tiny and cheap, comes in 3V or 5V variants, does not have serial port	3, 5	Arduino/C variant
Gemma	$9.95	Tiny and sewable, does not have serial port	1, 3	Arduino/C variant
Flora	$14.95	Fully compatible, great for wearable (or sewn) projects, has serial port	4, 8	Arduino/C variant

NAME	PRICE	BEST FOR	# OF ANALOG AND DIGITAL PINS	LANGUAGE
Photon	$19	WiFi-enabled, RGB LED status light, has SDK to control or wirelessly program from a smartphone	6, 8	Arduino/C variant
LightBlue Bean	$34.95	Bluetooth enabled, has accelerometer, temperature sensor, and RGB LED on board, has mobile app to control or wirelessly program it	2, 6	Arduino/C variant, wireless programming

Based on your circuit diagram and user flow, you can purchase the exact components you need to build out the prototype. Make sure to buy a couple of each component because it's pretty easy to break some of the smaller and more fragile ones.

Here is a list of my favorite resources for purchasing components.

The best designed, easiest to use shops with tutorials:

- Adafruit (*www.adafruit.com*)
- SparkFun (*www.sparkfun.com*)
- Maker Shed (*www.makershed.com*)

The more technical shops:

- Jameco (*www.jameco.com*)
- All Electronics (*www.allelectronics.com*)
- AliExpress (*http://bit.ly/2gPCd3K*)
- eBay—if you know exactly what you need

For custom circuit boards:

- OSH Park (*https://oshpark.com*)

Low-Fidelity Physical Prototypes

Prototype fidelity levels aren't quite as clear cut as they appear to be for digital products. Low fidelity for physical products might seem more like a mid-fidelity due to having actual, physical components that you connect together instead of merely having paper as a medium. The nature of electronic components gives these prototypes a more well-defined experience from the user's point of view—they're physical from the first prototype. What's more difficult about prototyping at a low fidelity is that your idea is still in its early stages. So it's best to introduce low-fidelity physical prototypes with the proper expectation setting of where you are in your idea development.

BREADBOARDING

A great low-fidelity prototype you can start with, and my favorite way to prototype circuits, is using a breadboard (a solderless construction base for building electronic circuits) with a microcontroller (Figure 6-20). You can use small lengths of solid core wires with the ends stripped (as opposed to stranded wire that's made up of many smaller strands) or jumper wires, and plug the ends into the breadboard and the microcontroller. It's important to use solid core, or to solder the tips of a stranded core wire, to make it easy to plug in and pull out of the breadboard. Believe me, it's no fun to try to stuff a flexible, stranded core wire into a specific, tiny point on the board!

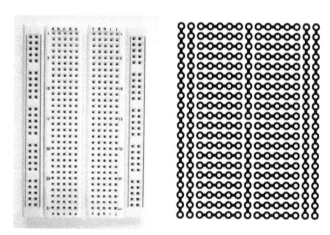

FIGURE 6-20

A breadboard allows you to make solderless circuits, right is how the inner board is connected for the power columns, and numbered rows

Sometimes it's helpful to use a microcontroller that has headers so you can plug it into the breadboard, such as the one shown in Figure 6-21. Or you can solder headers onto any other microcontroller to make it easier to rapidly prototype circuits.

FIGURE 6-21
A Trinket microcontroller with and without headers

The Arduino Uno is a great option for a beginning microcontroller due to its price ($25), availability worldwide, and online community. Arduino, the company, is an open source electronics platform that sells a variety of different microcontrollers, has a very supportive community and well-documented products. The Uno is great for low-fidelity prototypes because it already has headers on it and you can make circuits without soldering by plugging wires into the Uno directly and using a breadboard to build out the rest of the circuit (Figure 6-22).

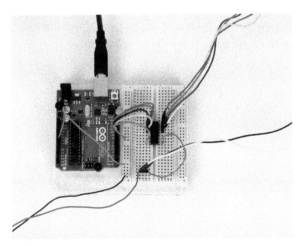

FIGURE 6-22
An Arduino Uno with a breadboard

For example, if I'm creating an email notifier that changes an LED's color every time I get a new email, I would build two different circuits to test it at a low fidelity. One circuit would set up the LED and have the code to change the color randomly, and the second circuit, or really only code, would get the email number from my computer and transfer it to the Arduino. Figure 6-23 shows what the circuit diagram looks like.

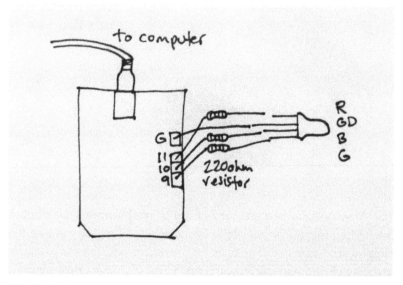

FIGURE 6-23
Circuit diagram for an email notifier

And Figure 6-24 shows what my breadboard looks like. In the top circuit, I added two buttons to "fake" when it receives an email and when the email is read, turning the lights on and off, so I could test the code. The bottom circuit is the final version for the email notifier.

FIGURE 6-24
Breadboards with the LED in place

Now I need to write the code for these two parts in order to test this idea.

To get started with breadboarding, you can purchase starter kits from the Adafruit website or Arduino website, and learn more about the basics of Arduino in *Arduino in a Nutshell* (O'Reilly). If you don't want to buy a whole kit, it's helpful to purchase at least a few of the common components, as stated in the preparation portion of this chapter. Once you're up and running, you'll be able to create lots of different circuits with minimal additional supplies and with ease.

CODE FOR ARDUINO

In addition to building the actual circuit, you'll need to write code for the microcontroller. There is already so much written online that will help you figure out how to write the code you need, and to get you most of the way there by using open source examples. Arduino is a good place to start because of its robust community and history. You'll be able to find many project examples with code for you to build off of so that you don't have to start from scratch.

Code for Arduino microcontrollers is written in a very specific way using a simplified version of the C++ programming language. It's saved in files called "sketches" (not to be confused with the design program Sketch), and other microcontrollers can be a little different, so I'll focus on Arduino primarily for this book (see Figure 6-25). You'll need to download the Arduino software, and connect your microcontroller to the computer in order to transfer code to it. I'll give you a quick overview so that you understand what we're working with. If you want to go deep into coding, check out these books:

- *Programming Arduino: Getting Started with Sketches* by Simon Monk (McGraw-Hill)

- *Make: Electronics* by Charles Platt (Maker Media)

- *Arduino Cookbook* by Michael Margolis (O'Reilly)

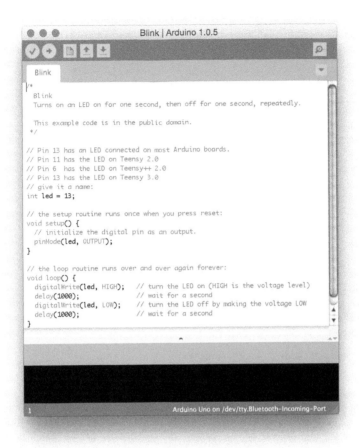

FIGURE 6-25

Arduino's integrated development environment (IDE)

The three main parts of a sketch are the variables, the setup, and the loop (Figure 6-26). See Figure 6-27 for an example sketch that turns an LED on and off, called Blink. Variables are a way to name and store a value that you can reference later in the loop. You have to declare them specifically at the beginning of the code so that the microcontroller knows what you're referring to when you tell it to do something to the variable. The most common variable you'll use is an integer. An integer can store a whole number–based value and associate a name with that value. You'll notice in the Blink sketch (Figure 6-27) we declared an integer value for the LEDpin. Now we know which pin number we're referring to later in the code.

```
#add some libraries

int /*set up some variables*/ = set

void setup () {
    //set up some stuff
    variable = 23
}

void loop () {
    //the good stuff
    if (something)
    {
        do this to variable
    }
    else if (something else)
    {
        do this instead to variable
    }
    else ()
    {
        this will happen
    }
    other actions such as saving variable
}
```

FIGURE 6-26
The basics of code—variables, setup, loop

```
int led = 13; //says that there's an LED connected to pin13

// the setup routine runs once when you press reset:
void setup() {
  // initialize the digital pin as an output.
  pinMode(led, OUTPUT);
}

// the loop routine runs over and over again forever:
void loop() {
  digitalWrite(led, HIGH);    // turn the LED on (HIGH is the voltage level)
  delay(1000);                // wait for a second
  digitalWrite(led, LOW);     // turn the LED off by making the voltage LOW
  delay(1000);                // wait for a second
}
```

FIGURE 6-27
The Blink sketch

You can include libraries at the top of your code that save you time by utilizing preset code for specific components (Figure 6-28). Adafruit provides many libraries for its different components so that it's faster to make something with them. Their RGB LEDs work with a library that already has a rainbow mode and random color generation built into it.

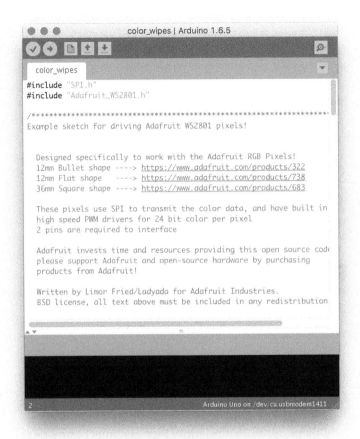

```
● ● ●                    color_wipes | Arduino 1.6.5
✓ ● ▣ ⬆ ⬇                                                          🔎

 color_wipes                                                         ▼
#include "SPI.h"
#include "Adafruit_WS2801.h"

/*****************************************************************
Example sketch for driving Adafruit WS2801 pixels!


  Designed specifically to work with the Adafruit RGB Pixels!
  12mm Bullet shape ----> https://www.adafruit.com/products/322
  12mm Flat shape   ----> https://www.adafruit.com/products/738
  36mm Square shape ----> https://www.adafruit.com/products/683

  These pixels use SPI to transmit the color data, and have built in
  high speed PWM drivers for 24 bit color per pixel
  2 pins are required to interface

  Adafruit invests time and resources providing this open source code
  please support Adafruit and open-source hardware by purchasing
  products from Adafruit!

  Written by Limor Fried/Ladyada for Adafruit Industries.
  BSD license, all text above must be included in any redistribution

▲▼

 2                                     Arduino Uno on /dev/cu.usbmodem1411
```

FIGURE 6-28
A library being called in code at the top

The setup is run once at the beginning of the program, and indicates the starting value for each of your variables (if needed) and any other things that need to be initialized before you get to the loop code.

The loop is the meat of the code where we tell the microcontroller what to actually do. It's called a loop because it will repeat itself over and over again, until you tell it to stop or until your device runs out of power. You can write many different things in this area: if/then statements (similar to an "if this then that"), basic math, reading sensors, and writing outputs. It's up to you to invent what you want this microcontroller to do.

For a more detailed walk-through of a sketch, check out this tutorial from Arduino (*https://www.arduino.cc/en/Tutorial/Sketch*).

PSEUDOCODE

One helpful trick I use when working on prototype code is to write out what I want to happen in pseudocode first. *Pseudocode* is a storytelling approach to coding. It's similar to writing out a user flow for your electronic device, but it's more detailed in the actual aspects of the story. Dig into the real inputs and outputs you have, and how those inputs are used. Pseudocode is where you can start figuring out some of the math that the loop of your code will have to do. You'll quickly determine how many pins you're using, if the pin needs to be digital or analog, and how often you want the loop to run.

For example, if I revisit the email notifier that changes the color of an LED each time you receive and email, the pseudocode story I write might look like this:

Check how many new emails I have.

Take that number and see if it's more or less than the previous email count.

Take action depending on the result:

- If it's more, I have new emails, so turn on the LED or change the color of the LED.

- If it's less, I must have read some emails, so turn the light off.

- Otherwise, if it's the same, then nothing has happened, so don't do anything.

Save the new email number to use next time.

Now that I have the story written out, I can see that I need to save the number of emails as a variable so that I can reuse it in the next loop, I will need to do some math on the email numbers, and I will need an if/else statement to determine which output happens. Now I can do a bit of Googling to help find the chunks of code that will fill in these blanks.

There is a huge online, open source community for Arduino microcontroller code and projects. You can find almost any type of project and at least some code to start with, and you're encouraged to build off of it and improve it! It's helpful for the community if you share back your work to help continuously improve the available projects online.

For my email notifier example, I searched for a project that pulled email numbers from Gmail. I found the ardumail project (*https://github. com/RakshakTalwar/ardumail*) that helped me with my base code.

Accessing an email count requires writing in Python, a high-level, general-purpose programming language that works on operating systems. What's nice about Python is that it was designed to be readable, so you can understand the functions that are happening by reading it. When I built this project, I had not used Python before, and I was able to take the code snippet from the previous project and tweak it to work for mine. You'll learn quickly how to hack other projects to make it work for your own.

This script, shown in Figure 6-29, resides on a computer and, using the computer's WiFi, logs into your Gmail account, checks the number of emails, and sends that number to the Arduino through the serial port, if connected by cord, or through WiFi or Bluetooth. You could use a WiFi-enabled microcontroller like the Raspberry Pi and eliminate the need for a computer. You'll still need the Python script, though, to log in and check your email.

The Arduino itself does all the math (Figure 6-30). You can see that I have a few different variables so that the Arduino can do the math, and I've set up the outputs and serial port. The variables include:

ledPin
> The LED that will change color each time I receive an email

val
> The value that the Arduino receives from the serial port

emailnumber
> The initial value for that number, which will be replaced when I receive a number from the serial port

lastemailnumber
> The variable that we'll use at the end of each loop to save the email number so that we can compare it to the new email number in the next loop

Keep in mind the specific constraints on how to name variables; the name must be one word without spaces.

check-gmail.py

```python
import serial, sys, feedparser, time
#Settings - Change these to match your account details
USERNAME="YOUR EMAIL ADDRESS example bob@gmail.com"
PASSWORD="YOUR PASSWORD"
PROTO="https://"
SERVER="mail.google.com"
PATH="/gmail/feed/atom"
# PATH="/gmail/feed/atom/Bills" # for specific GMAIL label

SERIALPORT = "/dev/tty.usbmodemfd141" # Change this to your Arduino serial port

# Set up serial port
try:
    ser = serial.Serial(SERIALPORT, 9600)
except serial.SerialException:
    print "no device connected - exiting"
    sys.exit()

var = 1
while var == 1 :  # This constructs an infinite loop
    newmails = int(feedparser.parse(PROTO + USERNAME + ":" + PASSWORD + "@" +
        SERVER + PATH)["feed"]["fullcount"])
    # Output data to serial port
    if newmails == 1:
        ser.write("a")
        #ser.write("FLAG")
        #print "some mail"
        print newmails

    if newmails == 2:
        ser.write("b")
        #ser.write("FLAG")
        #print "some mail"
        print newmails

    if newmails == 3:
        ser.write("c")
        #ser.write("FLAG")
```

Line 1, Column 1   Tab Size: 4   Python

FIGURE 6-29

Python script for the email notifier

FIGURE 6-30

The Arduino code for the email notifier

The setup includes setting the `ledPin` to be an output (as opposed to an input), and starting our serial monitor. Within the loop, you can see the math that the Arduino does for us. The last part of the Arduino code saves the `emailnumber` as the `lastemailnumber` before it repeats its loop. These statements align exactly with the pseudocode we wrote previously, but now it's in the proper syntax and code.

Open source code and tutorial projects are all over the internet. You can find the code that you need by just Googling, or you can check out some of my favorite places to learn specific electronics code:

- Instructables (*www.instructables.com*)
- Adafruit's learning platform (*learn.adafruit.com*)
- SparkFun's tutorials (*learn.sparkfun.com*)
- Arduino's tutorials (*http://bit.ly/2gNp7Ek*)
- Makezine (*makezine.com/projects*)

New sites pop up all the time for electronics tutorials, so you'll want to keep your eye out for inspiring projects. Make sure to check out these makers to see how they're pushing the boundaries on prototyping and creating with this level of electronics:

Anouk Wipprecht
A fashion–tech designer who combines microcontrollers, futuristic 3D printing, and high fashion together to create beautiful, wearable experiences.

Richard Clarkson Studio
An experimental furniture, lighting, and product studio that creates and invents whimsical and wonderful electronics products including the Cloud and Saber lamps.

Becky Stern
A master DIYer who combines electronics, wearables, and textile design to create awesome projects, often as tutorials on YouTube. She's previously worked at Make: and Adafruit, and is now a content creator at Instructables.

COMPONENT PROTOTYPES

Once you get the hang of building small circuits and writing basic code, you should prototype and test each of your main components individually before combining them together. This process allows you to better tackle troubleshooting, which you will always need to do. Some common issues you'll encounter when troubleshooting include: in code, using a colon instead of a semicolon or missing a bracket, and with the electronics, a poor solder joint, an improper power voltage, missing a resistor, or even a breadboard wire not being pushed in far enough.

Each component you add to a project increases the level of complexity and the number of aspects you have to check every time something goes wrong. By building an idea piece by piece, you can alleviate some of the worry, because you'll have your code solidly written, and you'll only have to check the transition points when you combine them together. This process is sometimes called unit tests in other fields. For our purposes, I call them component prototypes.

For example, I built the Chameleon Bag (shown in Figure 6-31), a smart messenger bag that can sense what's inside of it and what's missing, by combining an RFID sensor input (the same used for security badges) with a panel of 49 RGB LEDs (that can change color) for output. I always find myself leaving important items at home or at work, like my keys or cell phone, causing me to run back and be late for appointments. I needed a way to remind me of what I've forgotten, specifically, so that I don't leave without it. The final product had to be something that I would use every day, and functional beyond just reminding me what I forgot. Thus I decided to build a smart bag that would fit all of my personal gear, and still have room for the electronics too!

The RFID reader tracks what's inside of the bag, and can remind you if you've forgotten something through the LED's color and animation. The first prototype I made was to test the sensor input from the RFID reader. I wrote code for my Arduino to take that sensor input to test if it was working. Then on a separate Arduino, I connected and wrote code for the RGB LEDs to create different patterns, colors, and animations (Figure 6-32). Only after I had the two components working separately without bugs did I put them together and combine both sets of code into a final form (Figure 6-33).

FIGURE 6-31

The Chameleon Bag warns if you've left something behind

FIGURE 6-32

I first wrote the code for the RGB LEDs

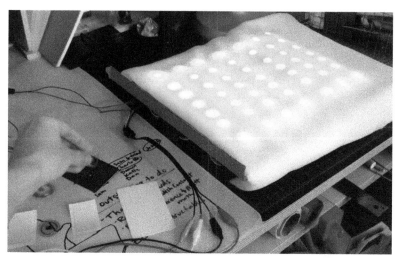

FIGURE 6-33

Then I connected the LEDs with the RFID reader for testing

An alternative way to prototype components is to create an analogous prototype to test an idea. You don't necessarily need the real components to test the code and viability of an idea, especially if your components are expensive or large. Instead, you can build a low-fidelity prototype using stand-ins for the real components.

For example Lisa Woods, an interaction designer, wanted to create a large-scale experience where visitors could turn plate-sized dials to change the color of a huge, projected mural. Instead of starting with plate-sized dials, she worked with a small potentiometer and a single RGB LED (Figure 6-34).

This analogous prototype has the same interaction pattern, but is a more reasonable scale to test the viability first. If she had discovered that the idea wasn't interesting enough, or didn't work for her audience, she could have pivoted the project without much loss. After completing this prototype, she was able to use the code with alternative components and build out a larger version closer to scale (Figures 6-35 and 6-36).

FIGURE 6-34

Lisa Woods built an analogous prototype to test her idea without investing in large-scale materials

FIGURE 6-35

The potentiometer prototype evolved into a clock-hand interaction for the installation

FIGURE 6-36

Digital Dreamer, the final, large-scale installation by Lisa B. Woods, Ryan Padgett, Sarah Thomas, and Kevin Reilly

Mid-Fidelity Physical Prototypes

Most of your physical prototypes will reside in the mid-fidelity range. There are a few areas that allow you to increase fidelity, but you might need multiple prototypes to achieve the full experience of your product. I'll show a few examples of how to build prototypes that will help you communicate specific design intents, or test your assumptions and the functionality of your idea.

COMPONENT PROTOTYPES

Similar to low-fidelity component prototypes, you can use multiple, less complex prototypes to test one larger idea. It will help you to move faster if you can test individual parts of your product's experience instead of waiting until you can build out a full, more perfect representation of how your product works.

At this point in your process, you'll still be using larger electronic components that can be breadboarded or soldered to create your prototype. Since you'll have people interact with these prototypes, you'll need to make your connections more robust. If you're using a breadboard, secure your connections with a bit of tape or place the whole microcontroller and board into an enclosure. If you're soldering, make sure your solder joints are solid, and use heat shrink tubing around the joints for extra support (Figure 6-37). As you prototype more, you'll learn the balance between amount of time spent building the prototype and the robustness needed for your particular test.

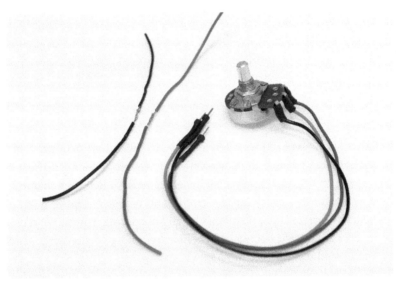

FIGURE 6-37
Left: bare solder joints; right: heat shrink tubing to cover solder

To give an example, I'll take you deeper through the prototyping process for Tempo, a haptic pacing armband (Figure 6-38). During development, I created six levels of prototypes, each one testing a unique part of the product. The original goal of the armband was to increase productivity by helping the user focus on the task at hand through a haptic rhythm. I had many assumptions to test to prove the viability of this goal.

FIGURE 6-38
The finished Tempo band

The first prototype I made was to test the circuit and setup of my components. I was unsure if the output of the vibration motor would be too distracting or electrical-feeling, so I used a small Trinket microcontroller and breadboard to try out the circuit and to test it (Figure 6-39). I tested a few different haptic motors to help me decide which one to use going forward, and it helped inform how to build a version on a band so that I could test the next version with users.

The second prototype is quick and cheap, and my goal with it was to test if the haptic sensation was viable or not on the user's arm (Figure 6-40). Since I used most of the code that I wrote for the first prototype, this prototype only took 15 minutes to make and cost less than $15. I used a Trinket microcontroller, a coin cell battery pack, one potentiometer, and two vibration motors. I tested this prototype with users to see if they had initial positive or negative reactions to having a pulsed pattern of vibrations. I made a loose band so that the user could wear this early model and give better feedback.

FIGURE 6-39
I built a test circuit
with a Trinket and
breadboard

FIGURE 6-40
The second prototype tested if the haptic sensation was viable on the user's
arm

By using this prototype, I might have learned that users completely hated the sensation; and then I could have pivoted the project with little loss of time or money. However, from testing the band with users, I learned that they were open to the haptic output, so I moved on to the next prototype.

The third prototype is a little more refined (Figure 6-41), allowing me to carry it around and get feedback from many people. My goal was to test the specific pacing rates and to find a default pattern to ship with the product. I designed the prototype to have a few users wear it for a longer period of time to see how it affected their working rate and other activities.

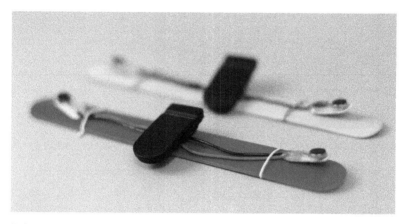

FIGURE 6-41
The third prototype tested specific pacing rates

I used the same Trinket microcontroller and vibration motors, but I learned from the previous prototype that I needed to reinforce the wires so that the prototypes would last longer and stand up to continual use (Figure 6-42). I used slap bracelets for the band so that it was easy for the users to put on and use.

One insight I learned is that at a specific rate, the pulsing had the same pattern as a cell phone ringing, and that sensation was unnerving for the user. I changed the cadence of the vibrations for future prototypes because of that reaction. Another insight was how users put the prototypes in surprising places (Figure 6-43). Most put it on their wrist, lower arm, or upper arm, but a few put it on their ankle and forehead. These interactions prompted me to consider designing a more flexibly sized band that could accommodate different placements on the body.

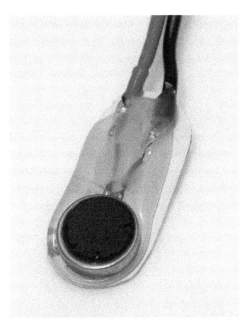

FIGURE 6-42
I reinforced the
vibration motors with
hot glue

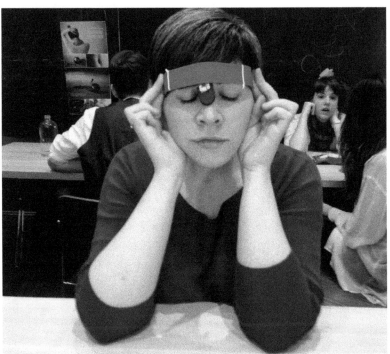

FIGURE 6-43
Users put the prototype in surprising places

Based on the user feedback of wanting direct control over the pulse rate, I included input dials in the fourth prototype. The goal for this prototype was to see how the user would control the length of the pulse, and the length of the pauses between the pulses (Figure 6-44). I used an Arduino Micro, a smaller, more robust microcontroller, with two potentiometers. Instead of having the whole setup on the armband, I added long wires to the armband and vibration motors, and had the "control panel" separate. Although the final product would not look like this, by having a lower fidelity visual, I was able to better test the interaction of the prototype. I gave this prototype to a few different users to incorporate into their work process, and let them control the pulsing.

FIGURE 6-44
This prototype allowed the user to change the pulse length, front and back sides of the controller

The added control was a huge hit with my users. They played around with the dials until it was a perfect rate and gave feedback that they wanted to save their favorite patterns so that they could go back to them depending on the activity they were doing (Figure 6-45). I was able to incorporate that feedback into the app design that I was working on simultaneously.

A surprising insight from this round of testing was the variety of different activities for which each individual wanted to use the armband. A few examples include meditation, yoga, pacing a run, as a silent metronome, and as a therapeutic device for carpal tunnel. Because of this feedback, I widened the scope of my use cases to include productivity, sports, music, and therapy. By user testing my prototypes, I found a wider audience for my product, and learned new ways to promote it. The market expanded, helping me understand the value that this device could bring, and the bigger scope for marketing and selling it. Based on this feedback, I had more assumptions to test for how the product would be used in these different activities.

FIGURE 6-45
The users really enjoyed controlling and changing the pulse patterns

The fifth prototype was a material study for a sports use case (Figure 6-46). I was originally designing a band to be worn at an office, or in normal, everyday situations. Reframing that use case into a sports use was an interesting challenge. My goal for this prototype was to test aesthetics and comfort through materials. I explored a few different types of material, including silicon and neoprene. Both are easy to clean and regularly used for skin-based applications. I chose to make the prototype with neoprene due to its comfort level and flexibility. It's regularly used to make orthopedic braces, so I wanted to test it for my armband.

I placed hard cardstock inside of the band to imitate the electronics that would be in the final product. I chose colors for the details, and notions including metal loops. I sewed the velcro onto the neoprene, and then used rubber cement to hold the two layers of neoprene together. When you're building non-functional prototypes, you have to hack it together the best that you can. The important part, if you're testing aesthetics, is that it looks like your final product idea.

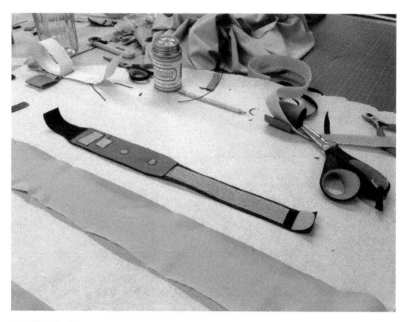

FIGURE 6-46
I used neoprene for the materials based on a sports use case

I had users wear this prototype during their activities and rate the comfort level of the material on their skin. They wore it during runs and yoga to test the viability of the use case (Figure 6-47). I got feedback that pulling the band through and folding it was not ideal, and that it was a bit bulky. For the next iteration, I worked on sourcing thinner components and thinking through alternative ways to make a flexibly sized, comfortable band.

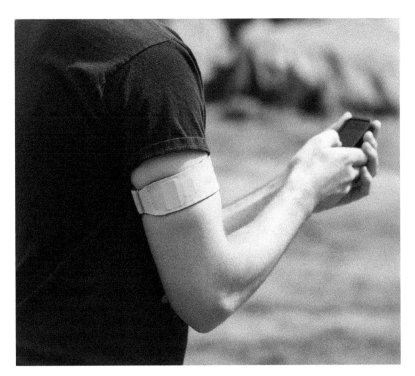

The users tested the material prototype by running and doing yoga

The sixth prototype pulled all the insights gathered from the previous five together with the final materials and capability (Figure 6-48). My goal was to interact and wear this final prototype for extensive periods of time and across different activities. I used smaller components and a rechargeable battery with a Bluetooth microcontroller so that I can adjust the pattern with my smartphone.

With this prototype, I tested long-term use with myself and with a few users. I regularly wear this prototype when I present at conferences and talks to help me talk at a slow pace, as directed by the pulse of the band, and it helps me remember to breathe while speaking to large groups of people.

FIGURE 6-48
The final prototype combined all the testing results into a fully functional product design

I'm still learning from this prototype, and it's made me look more professional in my conversations with investors and manufacturers. I often hear my audience say they'd like to steal my prototype, which is a good reaction because that means they'll buy the product. I've been able to successfully talk with electrical engineers and manufacturers by using these prototypes as the center of our meetings and conversations. It's much easier to source production-level components when you can point to the larger, hobby-sized version in action.

Each of these prototypes improved my product in a unique way, and built upon each other in order to validate the original use case, create new use cases, and be fully functional and ergonomic. I would not have been able to make this final prototype from scratch without the iterative, user-centered process that I employed. The next steps to develop this prototype into a product are to develop manufacturing-ready specs and work with companies to source the parts and labor to make an initial run of the product.

ADDITIONAL EXAMPLES

A similar process of prototyping through many versions is utilized by the creators of all sorts of smart objects and Internet of Things products. One example is the Hammerhead smart bike navigator (Figure 6-49). This team went through countless iterations before deciding on the functions, form, and application design for their product. You can see in the figure that they started with very low-fidelity prototypes of the LED indicators. The users being able to understand the directions the lights indicate is the most valuable part of the product, and the first thing that they focused on.

FIGURE 6-49
Hammerhead
prototypes

After establishing the LED arrangement, they began working on the casing (Figure 6-50). The team first tried a boxy case to cover the protoboard, but quickly added sanded plexiglass to diffuse the LEDs, making them easier to see and understand. They slowly updated their hardware—with different types of LEDs and microcontroller—and designed a sleek, curved housing. Eventually, they had their own printed circuit boards (PCB) made, and casing manufactured to the perfect spec for the product (Figure 6-51).

FIGURE 6-50

The Hammerhead team created a low-fidelity housing to test their idea with more context

FIGURE 6-51

After testing at lower fidelities, the Hammerhead team created a high-fidelity circuit board and casing

Another example is IDEO's ground-breaking user-centered design work on the Diego medical device, a powered tissue dissector for ear, nose, and throat surgeries. Their design team worked directly with surgeons and engineers to understand existing tools, current problems, and how to design something feasible to make. They observed how surgeons used existing technology to find pain points in their process and current tools. A few insights they gained from their contextual inquiry on the current tool were that its cords often got tangled, it regularly got clogged, and that the operators would get fatigued after using it for extended periods of time.

During a work session with six surgeons, designers grabbed materials from around the room and taped them together to make a physical prototype based on the surgeons' feedback (Figure 6-52). The surgeons were then able to handle the low-fidelity prototype, and shared their thoughts on the ergonomics of the proposed device. The team's goal was to create a comfortable handle that was easy to manipulate and use for longer periods of time, and the prototype they made allowed them to discuss their idea in further detail with the surgeons on hand.

FIGURE 6-52
While working with surgeons, designers co-created a prototype of the Diego medical device with found materials (photo courtesy of IDEO)

Their final product was a huge success (Figure 6-53). It ended up reducing the duration of procedures, limiting the amount of anesthesia the patients needed to be exposed to. The new Diego device tripled the company's revenue and increased its market share by 16%.[1] It's greatly advanced the medical procedures, and enabled faster recuperation times for its patients. Prototyping at a low- and mid-fidelity level allowed IDEO's designers to communicate with their clients and understand how they would use the final device.

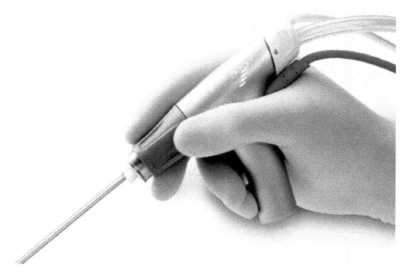

FIGURE 6-53
The final Diego device tripled the company's revenue and increased its market share (photo courtesy of Olympus)

ITERATIVE IMPROVEMENTS

As you iterate and build more prototypes, you need to employ a few additional tricks to improve and to make more robust prototypes.

---

1   "Diego Powered Dissector System," Diego Powered Dissector System, accessed January 10, 2016, *https://www.ideo.com/work/diego-powered-dissector-system*.

Soldering

The first skill you should strengthen is your soldering prowess. The best way to get better at soldering is to practice extensively. When I taught myself soldering, I watched a bunch of YouTube videos to see exactly how the final joints should look and work, and then I tried it out on scrap wire. With additional practice, I was able to solder faster, with consistently good joints.

You need a few pieces of equipment before you start: a soldering iron, solder, and exhaust fan are the required pieces, but you might also want a set of helping hands, clips, and tools to work with wire like a cutter, stripper, and needle-nose pliers (Figure 6-54).

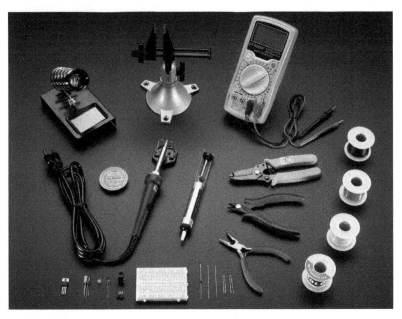

FIGURE 6-54

Setup of soldering equipment (*https://www.adafruit.com/products/136*)

To get started with soldering, check out this Instructable (*http://bit.ly/2gPEbkK*) or watch some of the thousands of videos online. It's much easier to learn by seeing and doing than by reading. Then, try soldering different types of wires (solid or threaded cores) and soldering on discarded circuit boards, perf- or protoboards (prototype boards with copper-plated holes to solder wires and components onto). It takes practice to get that perfect little hill on the metal pad, so buy extra perfboards to learn on before you solder your final components together (Figure 6-55).

FIGURE 6-55
It takes practice to be able to quickly solder quality joints

Protoboards

After you've tested your circuits on a breadboard but before you're ready to have a custom circuit board printed, you might want to make a sturdier circuit for your prototype. The best way to do that is to solder your wiring and components on protoboards. There are two different kinds of protoboard: perfboard and stripboard (Figure 6-56). The former is a grid of individual holes, each with its own copper solder pad. The latter has rows of holes connected to the same solder pad, similar to how a breadboard works. You can even buy protoboards that look exactly like a breadboard, but are thinner and allow you to solder wires to them.

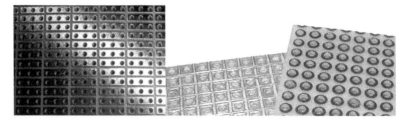

FIGURE 6-56
The two different types of protoboards are perfboard and stripboard, respectively

For most cases, I usually cut a piece of protoboard that will hold my circuit, arrange my wires (bending the ends to hold them in place; see Figure 6-57), and solder everything onto the back pads. I can then connect my microcontroller to the protoboard either by soldering it directly; soldering headers to the board so I can plugin or remove the microcontroller; or soldering wires that will connect to a separate microcontroller housing.

FIGURE 6-57
Bend your wires behind the protoboard to make it easier to solder in place

Copies

Once you get the hang of soldering circuits, the final tip I have for you is to make multiple copies of your prototypes, especially when the stakes are high for that specific test (Figure 6-58). I've had prototypes break on me just before, during, and right after user tests; wires detach, solder joints break, or something inexplicably goes wrong and it's impossible to figure out why. It's frustrating and sad to see all your hard work explode due to an unexpected drop or just plain bad luck. To give yourself peace of mind, and to be prepared for anything, make a second or third copy of your prototype to have in reserve.

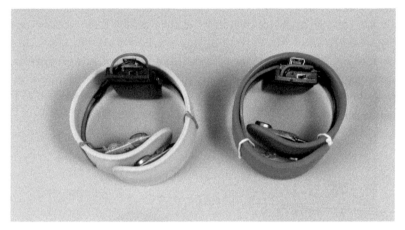

FIGURE 6-58
It's helpful to make multiple copies of a prototype, just in case one breaks during testing

If your prototype breaks mid-test, instead of canceling the rest of the session, you'll be able to go with the flow and pull out the backup. The value of the extra prototype greatly outweighs the extra time that it takes to build, as it doesn't take as much time as the first to build a copy. Finally, if your prototypes don't break, you can have two teams testing at the same time, covering more users and getting further feedback.

In some situations, it might not be financially feasible to make a copy (if you have very expensive components or is you are on a very tight deadline). In those cases, be extra certain that your solder joints are strong and consider adding additional support and structure with heat shrink tubing or hot glue to ensure your components don't break mid-test (Figure 6-59).

FIGURE 6-59
Make sure your prototypes are robust enough to stand up to testing by using heat shrink tubing and hot glue to reinforce joints

High-Fidelity Physical Prototypes

High-fidelity prototypes combine all the work you've done iteratively designing your physical product idea. You're now ready to create an electronic prototype with higher visual, breadth, depth, interaction, and data model fidelities. Before, you might have focused on one or two of these dimensions to test your specific assumptions. Now that you've tested those assumptions and improved your product, you can make a thorough prototype that covers more of the dimensions.

CUSTOM CIRCUIT BOARDS

You can order custom printed circuit boards (PCB) for your prototype or product online. A custom board has the exact spacing, solder pads, and peg holes you need for your specific electrical and surface mount components. These boards are usually smaller than a regular proto-board and are more polished and refined. There are low-cost online producers of circuit boards, including OSH Park (*https://oshpark.com*), by the same people who run SparkFun (Figure 6-60). This service will send you 3 copies of your board for $5 per square inch within 12 days. That's pretty awesome, and it gives you more control over your design and product.

FIGURE 6-60
You can order custom circuit boards from OSH Park at a reasonable price

You can design your circuit board using CADSoft EAGLE software, or other compatible CAD software. However, you can work with someone to help you make it if you're not interested or able to take on this level of technical work. At higher fidelity levels, it's helpful to collaborate or find support for the more complex and technical sides of developing a product. For detailed information on high-fidelity electronics, read *Prototype to Product: A Practical Guide for Getting to Market* by Alan Cohen (O'Reilly).

Another way to work with smaller, individual components is to solder a surface mount board (Figure 6-61). This type of board allows you to solder onto the surface of the board without needing peg holes, which results in a smaller overall circuit board. You will solder tiny components on top of solder pads using a thin soldering iron tip. It's an advanced skill that takes a lot of practice to master. You can shop out this kind of work to a local electrical engineer, or purchase built-out boards online.

FIGURE 6-61
A surface mount board doesn't have peg holes, so it can be smaller and use surface mount components

Once you have your custom PCBs printed and soldered, you can work on your product's outward appearance and detailed functions.

MATERIALS FOR HIGH FIDELITY

Higher-fidelity prototypes are a good area to try out and test your materials. Materials include the outer touch points and the inner support. In addition to materials, you can work toward finalizing your form factor and what materials make up each part of the product.

At this level, you can CNC-mill or 3D-print casings for your electrical components to better reflect the final form your product will take (Figure 6-62). There are some basic, free programs for 3D modeling, but you might want to collaborate with an experienced industrial designer or 3D modeler to help you create your printing file. If you're collaborating, sketch the general form of your product, taking into account the final sizes and shapes of your electrical components, in order to communicate your intent to your collaborator. Orthographic drawings will help, which is showing the shape from the front, side, and top to communicate the full three-dimensional form. You can create form studies with foam or cardboard as an additional communication tool.

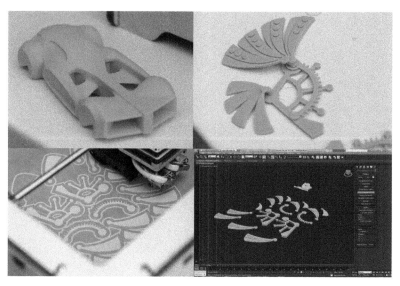

FIGURE 6-62

You can 3D-print your form to test the final shape and ergonomics

Once you have your 3D-printed form or milled shape, you can finish the surface. Most 3D models have a ribbed surface due to how they're printed layer by layer. You can sand the outside to a smooth finish, in order to better communicate injection-molded plastic or other types of manufacturing processes. If you have an alternative material—like fabric, leather, or wood veneer—cover the form with that material to best reflect the experience of the final product. For CNC-milled shapes, you might need a light sanding (if wood or medium-density fiberboard) or polishing (if metal), and then finish it with layers of paint, plastic dip, or patina.

Your material study can be functional or nonfunctional, depending on how small of components you're able to work with. Either way, make sure to test the object in its final setting, being used for its final purpose. If you're making a smart object for yoga practice, make sure it's tested in a yoga studio and get the reactions to both the material study and the functional prototype. You can present the material study to the user so that they understand how the product will look and feel, and then have them interact with the larger, bulkier electronic prototype, imagining that the functional version looks like the study.

POLISHED PRESENTATIONS

High-fidelity prototypes and material studies are an excellent way to present product ideas to business stakeholders and investors for consideration. This more refined work will give you more confidence in your idea and will show that you've thought through how the device will function, look, and behave. It shows a higher level of personal investment and commitment to the idea too. When you present your ideas with a high-fidelity prototype, make sure to include who your user is and what problem you're solving with your product. Investors aren't merely interested in the project revenue and net gain; they're looking for products that stand out, are differentiated, and have a clear purpose.

In the presentation, talk through your prototype's functions from the user's point of view. Set up a scenario that clearly explains the unique value to the user and how they would interact with it. Then share both a highly polished nonfunctional prototype and a potentially lower-fidelity functional prototype to show the full range of interactions. These presentations will help support your idea and win the support of your client or stakeholder.

MANUFACTURING

At this point in your process, and earlier on, you need to learn about manufacturing and how your prototype will be made as a final product. There are some major factors that you need to understand about how products are created at scale and how these final prototypes fit into existing manufacturing methods. One example is that an injection-molded plastic form cannot have undercuts and specific shapes because it must be able to pop out of its two-piece mold. You will also learn the balance between the cost of specific manufacturing methods and the type of finish they provide. Having a hand-carved wood housing may not be financially feasible for a large-scale electronic product. Or you might find that one small change to your product design will make it easier to assemble it, reducing the man-hours and cost of production by a significant amount.

This topic is a bit too in depth for this book, but luckily there are other resources that have covered it. *Mechanical Engineering for Hackers: A Guide to Designing, Prototyping, and Manufacturing Hardware* by Will McLeod (O'Reilly) gives a holistic view of how to create hardware projects, and *Prototype to Product: A Practical Guide for Getting to Market* by Alan Cohen (O'Reilly) gives a great complementary view of the product development process and how to overcome common pitfalls.

Troubleshooting

At some point in your physical prototyping process (or, if you rush through the process, often), your prototype will seem broken or not working properly. There are so many different things that can go wrong when you're building a physical prototype, and you'll need to be thorough and thoughtful as you build and as you troubleshoot.

Use these two checklists as a guide for troubleshooting when you can't figure out what's wrong with your prototype.

First, check your physical components. Ask yourself these questions:

- Are the connections all fully plugged in? Check the wires on your breadboard and your solder joints.

- Are the wires going to the proper pins? Double check your circuit to make sure everything is where it should be.

- Is your battery or power source providing power? Use a multimeter to check the wattage to make sure you're not giving it too much or too little power.

- Are any of your components overheating? Touch them lightly to see. You might need to add a heatsink if there's a heat problem.

- Is your prototype short circuiting? A short circuit means that some part of your circuit is allowing current, or power, to flow in an unintended path with little resistance. It can cause circuit damage, overheating, or even blow out some of your components. Check if wires are touching that shouldn't.

If it's still not working, check and debug your code. When you compile the code and send it to your Arduino, it should indicate if there's a problem. But there might be coding issues that the compiler doesn't pick up. Ask yourself these questions:

- Do you have any misspellings? Check your variable names and loop code.

- Did you mix up the code formatting? Check for semicolons and brackets. The compiler should pick this up, but it's always good to double check.

- Are all your necessary libraries called at the beginning of the code?

- Did you set up all the variables correctly?

One tiny change in code can break your prototype, so keep an eye on what you're doing. It can be very frustrating to have to troubleshoot throughout your process, but you'll slowly get the hang of checking as you go, and building stronger prototypes so that the physical side doesn't break down.

They Got It Right—Richard Clarkson

Richard Clarkson, creator and senior designer at Richard Clarkson Studio, knows all about prototyping, and employs it daily within his life and practice. His Brooklyn-based design laboratory regularly creates bespoke installations and products by experimenting with new technologies, and using traditional materials in different, innovative ways.

A prototype, to him, is anything that furthers the concept of an idea, and includes playing with materials and exploring new ideas through making. He often imagines product ideas in his head, then works through multiple prototypes to make improved versions of it a consumer-ready reality. Each step forward brings new polish to the idea, and each version of a product that he releases is another prototype, to be improved further in the future.

One of his most successful products is the Cloud Lamp (Figure 6-63). This lamp combines lighting with a Bluetooth speaker, audio visualization through RGB LEDs, and interaction with motion detectors. It is an impressive accomplishment, garnering international press and features in magazines such as *Fast Company*, *Urbis*, and *Wired*. However, this product didn't start as a perfect version, immediately ready to sell and mass-manufacture. Rather, it was developed through a series of prototypes and early versions that Richard created across four years of continuous work and evolution.

The very first embodiment of this idea resulted from an assignment for an MFA class to create a plush nightlight (Figure 6-64). Richard envisioned a light-up cloud lamp—fluffy and bright—as his solution to the prompt. In order to dig into the coding of his idea, using an Arduino, he combined some small yellow LEDs and a bit of fluff as his base. This prototype allowed him to learn and write the code he needed, testing out various flashing patterns and slowly adding features like storm sounds.

FIGURE 6-64

The first prototype combined a couple components to allow Richard to write the code and test his idea quickly

He refined the first version for the final class project, focusing on how to achieve the proper exterior fluff and adding functionality to the code and components (Figure 6-65). Instead of merely making a lamp with lights, Richard included a Bluetooth speaker and code to have the lights react to streamed music (Figure 6-66). He also included thunderstorms that would go off with a wave below the lamp, thanks to a motion detector. This version 1.1 was a first attempt at felting fluff into a cloud-like shape and texture, resulting in a shaggy look. Although he wasn't fully satisfied with the aesthetic, he had to finalize this version, and then make improvements in the future. He published blog posts and videos of the lamp in action, which garnered quite a buzz on social media and design blogs.

FIGURE 6-65
His next step was to build out the full functionality in the first smart Cloud

After the press and recognition that his Cloud 1.1 lamp received, Richard was commissioned to create a series of Clouds for an installation at a local NYC restaurant. To create a series of lamps that would hold up to a longer installation in public, he decided to revisit and improve the design and robustness of the internal structure and fluffing style. His goal for the second version was to make it easier and faster to make (so far he had handcrafted each Cloud himself), clean up the code to make it more streamlined, and improve the fluffy exterior.

FIGURE 6-66
This version included a Bluetooth speaker with RGB LEDs

He experimented with alternative internal structure, this time using a larger block of foam carved roughly into the cloud shape with holes cut out of the inside to hold the electronics and speakers (Figure 6-67). He also sourced smaller, better components for the different parts of the Cloud—different lights that coordinated across all the clouds to create a thunderstorm effect in the space. By the end of the commission, Richard created eight functional clouds and a few small, non-lighted clouds to fill out the space (Figure 6-68).

FIGURE 6-67
Richard experimented with a new internal foam structure to hold the electronics and allow for better fluffing

FIGURE 6-68
The final group of Clouds were installed at Birdbath restaurant

The next version, or prototype, that Richard made was to show at Maker Faire in New York City, a festival celebrating the maker movement by gathering enthusiastic DIYers, technologists, and hobbyists. He decided to take the time to build an even better internal structure and updated the speaker system. Through the trial and error of the first two versions, he knew that he needed a more rigid structure beneath the foam exterior. This time around, he used wire mesh to build the general shape, allowing more space inside for larger electronics, while still providing the structure to hold it all securely (Figure 6-69). With the extra space, he integrated a new speaker with a subwoofer and better sound quality. He also added a remote receiver to the microcontroller in order to better control the light and functions.

FIGURE 6-69
The third version had a robust metal structure to hold the new speaker system

He built out prototypes of the remote and tested it before finalizing the details and building a case for it. The whole, final product was displayed in its own darkened corner to allow the passersby to appreciate the lightning show (Figure 6-70 and 6-71).

FIGURE 6-70
Richard showed the third version at Maker Faire in 2013

At this point, Richard realized he had evolved his original design—it was easier to make, more structural, used higher-quality components, and included a better user interface—and he then decided to productize it on his studio website. He wanted to streamline the manufacturing process a bit more with this version, and worked hard to add polish to his design while still maintaining a reasonable cost for materials and labor. He explored many alternatives to the wire-mesh structure from v3, and decided to create a mold to vacuum form a clamshell-like external structure (Figure 6-72). By using a template and the exact same shape for each Cloud, he and his employees were able to more efficiently assemble the Clouds.

FIGURE 6-71
He also handmade a remote to control the cloud effects

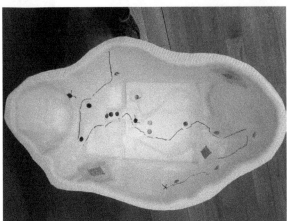

FIGURE 6-72
Richard streamlined his handmade Clouds with a vacuum-formed shell template with specific holes for LEDs and speaker outputs; the electronics fit into the shell perfectly

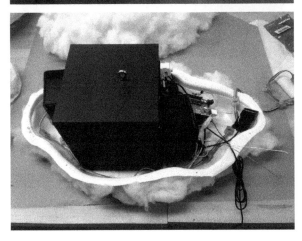

All his learnings about fluffing the exterior culminated in a specialized fluffing technique using hypoallergenic polyester fiber treated with a setting agent and a flame retardant. This process created a more durable exterior that does not allow the fluff to fall off or lose shape (Figure 6-73). Finally, Richard found a better IR remote to control the Cloud so that his product would look and feel more professional, and he would not have to make his own remotes long-term (Figure 6-74).

FIGURE 6-73
The final productized Cloud and remote began selling immediately on his website

FIGURE 6-74
He created a more polished remote

Since making these four different evolutions of the Cloud, and his success in selling them through his studio, Richard has expanded his product line to include quite a few additional Cloud versions. He still sells the Smart Cloud, though in sales volume its little brother Tiny Cloud has overtaken it. Recently he released an RGB version without speakers, in four sizes; a Cloud Shade version with more simplified lighting, also in four sizes; and a system of stands in a number of sizes and configurations (Figure 6-75).

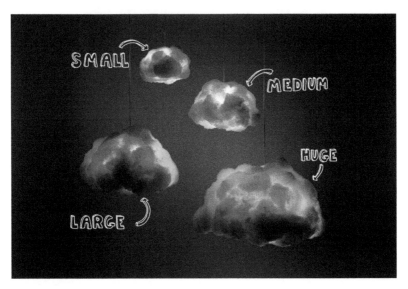

FIGURE 6-75
Richard now sells a variety of Clouds on his website

Richard's work on the Cloud product line has even created the opportunity to collaborate with other artists, musicians, technologies, and restaurants, including Mythology, Two Hands, Take 31, and Ursa Major. One collaboration resulted in a floating cloud, made with Crealev's levitation technology (Figure 6-76). He said the collaboration was somewhat seamless because he had worked out all the kinks within the Cloud, and it was a matter of combining two products together, like two component prototypes coming together in a final product. The proof of concept he created is the first step in potentially creating a new product to bring to market, but it needs more work to make a lighter base and to find better battery technology for the Cloud.

FIGURE 6-76
The floating cloud proof of concept is currently being made into a full product

Finally, Richard's exploratory work into various components on the Cloud allowed him to invent new ways to use electronics that didn't work out in the Cloud itself. One idea that was a branch off was Saber, a music and sound visualizer luminaire (Figure 6-77). Riffing off the Cloud's visualization code, Richard took it a step further by more accurately representing sounds though specific linear animations in the long, vertical light.

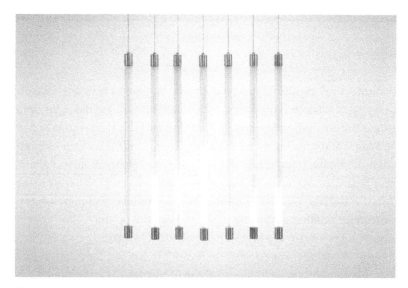

FIGURE 6-77
Saber takes sound visualization a step further than the earlier Clouds

Overall, in the journey to make the Cloud a reality, Richard took each version as an opportunity to try out new approaches to the structure, electronics, and external fluff aesthetic. He viewed each version as a prototype, even if someone was purchasing it. By putting his work out into the world before it was fully evolved, he found partners and commissions who wanted to be involved and part of the evolution process. He also created a more diverse product line based on his customers' reactions and the additional work he put into building out variations. He still incorporates experimentation and play into his everyday work in order to create new, innovative products and prototypes (Figure 6-78).

FIGURE 6-78
Richard in his studio

Summary

Prototyping for physical products has a few unique aspects, including material choices, tactility, electronics, and coding functionality. You can prepare yourself for success by creating a user flow and circuit diagram for your product. You can then purchase the electrical components you need to create your first prototype.

Starting with breadboarding, build out low-fidelity prototypes of your idea to test the functionality of your electrical components. It's simple to plug and create circuits with an Arduino Uno and a breadboard. You'll need to write code for the microcontroller you use, and use pseudocode to help you get started and understand what code to write. You can refer to the resources in the Appendix for finding tutorials and code to use for your projects.

Once you're up and running with building circuits, you can build individual component tests. By making prototypes of each component, you can be sure that it's functional and that its code works. By testing components individually, it will make it easier to combine them and to limit the hassle of troubleshooting later on.

Mid-fidelity and high-fidelity physical prototypes build on your initial circuit tests. With each iteration, your designs gain more polish and functionality. In your iterations, the fidelity level can increase for any of the five dimensions: visual, breadth, depth, interaction, and data model. As you begin making high-fidelity prototypes, you're ready to test materials and think about manufacturing. Find collaborators in these areas who can help you create or 3D print form studies. You can get help creating custom printed circuit boards and manufacturing files too.

With the guidance and resources in this chapter, you should feel empowered to try your hand at making electronic prototypes for your product ideas!

[7]

Testing Prototypes with Users

AFTER YOU'VE CREATED YOUR first, or hundredth, prototype and you want to test it, there's a bit of setup work you need to do. Testing with users is the process of getting someone who is as close to your ideal user as possible, and who is not you, to interact with your prototype to test a specific assumption or to find any pain points, problems, or confusion within your proposed idea. Observing a user directly interacting with your prototype will give you a wealth of information beyond "did the task get finished?" In person, you can look for microexpressions of frustration, delight, and confusion, and then ask follow-up questions to why the user felt that way. If you conduct testing remotely, you can listen for any hesitations and gain nearly as much insight into the question or assumption you're testing. Both in-person and remote testing provide quantitative and qualitative data that lets you examine the intuitive use and emotional response to an experience.

Planning the Research

The first step for successful user testing is to create a research plan that includes exactly what assumptions you want to test, the goal of the research, a few basic questions to establish who the test subject is, and the questions you need to ask or the tasks the user needs to accomplish to test the assumptions. This document can be formal, including a list of your stakeholders and business objectives that the test will affect, or it can be more casual, acting as a guide to help you during your testing. For a more formal version, look at Usability.gov's template (*http://bit. ly/2gPHWGK*). This formal version is helpful for high-visibility projects or projects with stringent nondisclosure agreements (NDA) or additional structures such as healthcare projects dealing with HIPAA compliance (protecting health information's confidentiality and security). I usually take a less formal approach for most of my prototype testing due to the less rigid structure I work in. I write out the goal and questions, which is usually enough guidance to successfully conduct my test.

ASSUMPTIONS AND GOALS

You might already know the assumptions you're testing because you designed the prototype to address those concerns directly. If you don't know which assumptions to test, start by writing out exactly how you expect your user to interact with the prototype or product and point out the most crucial tasks that the user will do in order to understand and use your product. Look back to your user flow, and see where there might be deviation points from your happy path. If you're later in the process, your assumptions will be more specific interactions and patterns.

Prioritize these assumptions in order to determine which ones are core to your solution, or must be true for your solution to fix the problem. Once you've determined the assumptions to test, write your goal for the research plan. If I'm making a meditation app, and my assumption is "users will be able to find the additional meditations in the hamburger menu," an example goal is "determine if a user can discover and choose a new meditation."

QUESTIONS

There are two types of questions you should ask your user: establishing questions and feedback questions. Establishing questions allow you to get to know this specific user, to understand their work background, and to find any hidden biases that may affect your testing. Here are some examples of the information you may want to gather:

- Name
- Job Description
- Team profile (if it's a work-based software)
- Home life (if it's a lifestyle product)
- What software/apps/smart objects do you use on a regular basis?
- What is your favorite app/smart object you've used recently and why?

- What's important to you when you think about [the goal of the product]

Establishing questions will help get the user comfortable talking with you and settled into the test. It's a great way to break the ice and allow them to open up about their background and interests. Sometimes I'll add in a fun question just to make everyone more comfortable. I'll ask about a favorite movie or television show. Or a favorite place they've traveled to. I won't use the answers for anything in particular, but it's a great way to get the conversation flowing.

Feedback questions are the meat of the interview, and should be written to accomplish your research goal. When you write these questions for your user testing, there are a few guidelines you should follow. The objective of these questions is to get your user to interact with your prototype in either an open or closed way, and talk about what they are doing, what they expect, and what issues they're having.

An open session is more exploratory and allows the user to interact and meander through the product. You might prompt them by saying "you've landed on this page (or received this physical product) and want to learn more about it or how to use it." Then let the user interact with the product in whatever way they see fit. This type of session is great for overall feedback on the experience, and seeing how a user might intuitively move through a new form of product. This type of session requires a higher breadth fidelity level, so that the user can try out the many different functions.

A closed session is a more guided approach and helps keep the user on track when you need them to complete more complex tasks or interactions that are specific to your goal. You will prompt the user with specific tasks throughout the session, telling them when they've completed a task and to start the next one. You might need a higher depth fidelity so that your user can fully dive into one function instead of lightly touching many. For a refresher on the different dimensions of fidelity, check out Chapter 3.

The biggest rule for writing research questions is to create open-ended, non-leading questions that do not result in "yes" or "no" answers. As Table 7-1 illustrates, you should frame your questions in an open-ended manner to keep the conversation—and insights—flowing.

TABLE 7-1. Ask open-ended questions that are not leading

DON'T ASK THIS	ASK THIS INSTEAD
Would you use this product?	How might this product integrate into your daily life?
Did you like feature "A"?	Observe how they interact with the feature; ask, "what did you expect to happen?"
Do you like this product?	What's your impression of this product?
What was your favorite thing about this product?	What were the top two things you liked and the top two things you disliked about this experience?

It takes practice to learn how to frame questions. For more insight into this specific area, check out *Just Enough Research* by Erika Hall (A Book Apart). She states that good questions are simple, specific, answerable, and practical. Once you write your questions, look at them objectively and determine if they're biased, leading, or off-topic. Take care in crafting your questions. Without proper framing, your users will not be able to give you good feedback.

Ask your coworkers to review your questions to find any additional hidden biases that you're no longer able to see. Red flags include yes/no questions, asking the user how they would solve the problem, or asking a user how much they would pay for the solution. These examples are asking your user to do your job for you! Try not to give too much information away, and let your users tell you what they want through their actions, not their words. What a user does usually differs from what they say that they do or will do. Keep an eye out for how they navigate, handle, or click on different parts of your prototype.

The more you can get the user to talk openly about the experience with your software or physical product, the more likely you'll find nuggets of insight and wisdom in what they're saying. More often than not, the most insightful conversations I have are usually right after the "testing" is done, and we're talking about what the user thought of the whole experience. So keep recording your conversation until you've left the room.

TASKS

Tasks are another way to guide the research so that you're testing your specific assumptions instead of letting a user go randomly through your product. Tasks should give the user a goal that aligns with the research goal, and then see if the user takes the assumed path to complete it. For the meditation app example, a task would be "sign into the service and choose a different meditation to listen to." It does not directly tell the user how to complete the task, only what they should accomplish. Don't give away too much information! You want to see if your user's actions match your assumptions.

A SAMPLE RESEARCH PLAN

Here's a sample research plan for the meditation app example:

Goals and assumptions

Determine if a user can discover and choose a new meditation

Assume that they will find the catalog of meditations in the menu and will be able to choose one based on the provided information

User profile

Beginner or intermediate experience with meditation

Has meditated at least once in the past week

Establishing questions

Name

Job description

What role does meditation play in your life?

How often do you meditate?

What existing meditation apps or products do you currently use?

How did you come to choose those apps or products?

Tasks

You are a returning user to this meditation app, and you'd like to find a new meditation that fits your current mood. Please select a new meditation.

Once you've "listened" to the meditation, you want to come back and use it later. How do you accomplish this?

Now that you've finished, what were the top two things you like about this experience, and what were the two things you disliked about it?

Conducting the Research

With your research plan in hand, you're ready to conduct your research. Now I'll cover some of the best practices, including how to find users and how to run the testing session.

FINDING USERS

The first thing you'll need to do is find users to test with. It may seem daunting to reach out to people to test a prototype, but I have a few tricks that make it easier.

The lowest barrier to users is to check with your friends and family to see if anyone fits your user persona. It's helpful for you to test with them first to get some initial research done, but remember that because of the nature of your relationship, they might not give you the hard, constructive feedback you need. Use them as an icebreaker to make sure your test is set up properly. Take their feedback with a grain of salt, and try to have additional non-relative users to back up any insights you gain. It's better to use friends for lower-fidelity prototypes that need bigger-picture feedback rather than high-fidelity work that looks too complete.

The best way I've found to engage and find specific users is to look for a meetup that your ideal user would attend, reach out to the organizers, and see if you can attend the next event. For our meditation app, it would be easy to attend any sort of meditation meetup and after it's done, ask the other attendees if they'd be interested in helping you with a project. You'll be surprised how many people love trying new products before they come out, and enjoy giving feedback to help you out. At these events, I gather emails from the people who are interested, and set up separate testing sessions with each.

If your user is the type that would work in a co-working space (entrepreneurs, start-ups, developers, etc.) you can pull off an intercept interview. I'll set up at a table with a sign asking for volunteers for testing sessions and timeslots that individuals can sign up for. A plate of cookies attracts people to the table, and a short conversation piques their interest enough to sign up (Figure 7-1). I then conduct the interviews in a private room at the assigned time. I sometimes provide an hono-rarium for these types of interviews too (see below).

FIGURE 7-1
You can set up at an open coworking space and entice potential users with treats to enlist their help

Other ways to find users are to put ads out on Craigslist or Facebook, or even place prototypes in the environment to get people to interact with them (this works best for outdoor smart objects). Practice caution when using these public means to find users. Make sure you conduct your research interview at a public place and that you don't go to the interview on your own.

You can pay for consultants to recruit users for you based on your spe-cific persona, for either in-person or remote testing. These recruitment firms are often costly and usually worth it only if you don't have direct access to a highly specialized user, such as an oncologist. Check with your company to see if you have a retainer with a recruiter already, or if they can provide one for your research work.

Some companies have users come into their offices on a regular basis for different teams to test new prototypes with. Etsy has a weekly time slot where they bring in either sellers or buyers, and their individual product teams can sign up to test with these users. The designers might not know what they need to test far in advance, but the frequent, routine access to users allows them to know they can test within a week when they need to.

You can reimburse your research participants for their time, especially if you have a high-power user persona such as a marketing analyst or a lawyer who are very short on time. The official term for this practice is *honorarium*, a payment given to a person who gives time in a "volunteer capacity or for services for which fees are not traditionally required."[1] There are some specific laws about honorariums for taxes and such, so you should do additional research if you decide to pursue paying your research participants. For high-level professionals, the consulting firm or recruiter will manage the honorarium payments. For other types of users, I recommend providing gift cards to places like Amazon or a local coffee shop to make it less transactional and more gratitude based.

Finally, you can use online user testing sites such as UserTesting.com to do remote testing (Figure 7-2). These tests can either be moderated by you or unmoderated. For unmoderated tests, the user performs the tasks, and their screen and voice are recorded so you can see and hear exactly how they tried to accomplish the task and what they were thinking while doing it. A benefit of using remote testing sites is that you can specify the exact type of person you'd like to test with, and you'll get a dispersed range of those people to interact with your prototype. The downside is that you don't have as much control over the quality of the test, especially if it's unmoderated, and you might not be able to follow up with the individual users to gain more insight into their reactions.

---

1 Wikipedia, "Honorarium," *https://en.wikipedia.org/wiki/Honorarium.*

FIGURE 7-2

UserTesting.com helps you test a broad range of people without needing them to be in person

RUNNING THE SESSION

Set up your research session for success by gathering the necessary materials before you start. You'll need your company's NDA or consent form for your user to sign, such as this one from Usability.gov (*http:// bit.ly/2gQP0mR*); the prototype; a way to record at least the audio, if not a video or screencast of the session; and ideally, a second person to take notes while you pose the questions and tasks (Figure 7-3). One easy way to record your screen is to use Quicktime or lookback.io. I try not to have more than two facilitators in the room with a user. If you have too many people, the user may be intimidated, and not comfortable enough to speak out loud. But it is very helpful to have two people: one to ask questions and follow-up questions, and a second to take notes based on the user's responses.

Gather your supplies and set up the test for success

Set up at least 30–60 minutes per user test in order to allow for enough time for the user to accomplish the tasks and discuss any additional questions and expectations they had afterwards.

At the beginning of the session, give your user a proper expectation of what you need from them: that there are no right or wrong answers, and you want to get real, honest feedback from the users in order to improve the product. Sometimes you'll come across a user who sugarcoats their feedback, and you'll have to really dig into what they're saying in order to discover any valuable insights. By starting out the session with an introduction to the user testing process, you'll be sure to get the user on board and giving usable feedback.

At the beginning of the session, ask for permission to record the session, and make sure you record from the beginning to the very end. Have your user think out loud as they go, so you can hear what they expected and what their initial reaction is to the content. If your user has never experienced thinking out loud before for a test, ask them to do a test round on a well-known website, like Amazon.com, and ask them to think aloud while they purchase a DVD. This activity should get them into the correct frame of mind so that you don't miss any insights. If during the testing you notice them go quiet for a bit, remind them to think out loud and ask what they were thinking about in that moment.

Keep an eye out for microexpressions, where the user looks confused, excited, frustrated, or even scared for a split second (Figure 7-4). If you are recording the user's face, you'll be able to analyze what they were doing at the moment their expression changed. Or you can dig deeper into those reactions to ask what they saw or thought then. You can ask what they expected to happen in that moment, and how that was different than what they experienced. Take notes, or have your teammate take notes, and return to the recording later to take supplementary notes about what the user enjoyed or disliked, and anywhere they got confused along the way.

FIGURE 7-4
Microexpressions can indicate subtle reactions to the product or experience

A common issue I've had to deal with is a user who gives solutions for the problems they see instead of focusing on the task itself. This type of user might get off task in order to solve a design obstacle; try to get them back on task with a bit of verbal support. "What would you do next to reach your goal?" is a great way to move them along.

Watch your body language and verbal cues during the testing to try not to give too many indications of whether the user is doing something correct or incorrect (Figure 7-5). In a test, there are no correct or incorrect answers, only reactions. Watch out for your own unintended verbal confirmations that will tell the user that there's a right and wrong way to accomplish the task. Your goal during the test is to neutrally observe the user's interactions and withhold any judgement or problem-solving until the synthesis of the findings.

FIGURE 7-5
Some body language indicates that there's a correct and incorrect way to accomplish the task

It's best to do at least four to eight user tests per prototype, or more for a very diverse audience or multiple personas, in order to find the common patterns that happen across most of the users. If strong patterns don't emerge, do additional tests, or rework some of your research plan to ensure that you're asking the right questions and presenting the proper tasks (Figure 7-6).

FIGURE 7-6
Conduct at least four to eight tests to observe how your users interacts with your prototype, where they get lost, and when they get frustrated

Synthesizing the Research

After the session, and preferably within a day, you're ready to find insights in your notes and recordings. Remember that if a user went off your happy path or had problems with the prototype, it's a good thing! You've found a problem that a user would have had with your finished product, but you found it before your product shipped. Finding areas of the product that you can improve is the main goal of prototyping and testing; it means the prototype was valuable.

Start by organizing your notes and writing anything that is potential feedback onto individual Post-it notes or in a list. After you've gone through the entire interview and you have a ton of Post-its, look over all of them and start grouping similar ideas into categories (Figure 7-7). These categories will tell you what can be improved in your prototype, and what you should ideate on next. Bring in your teammates to help with categorizing; there might not be obvious groupings, but you'll be able to see some clear directions on how to fix problems that users came across.

FIGURE 7-7
Sort all of your observations into categories to determine the main insights

Write out an insight for each of the categories. Some examples of insights include: the call to action text meant something different to each user, the user was unable to find a specific feature, and choosing the initial settings was easy and fast (insights can also be good!). The insight should indicate the problem area, or success area, without suggesting a solution yet (Figure 7-8). Based on the insight, think of lots of different solutions for those problems. Explore alternative user flows or navigation patterns. Think through different wording or visual design for your buttons. Use this space to create a recommendation on the direction you think the product and interactions should improve. Prioritize which insights and recommendations should be implemented into the next round of prototyping to test your updates.

Document your design decisions, with supporting user quotes and anecdotes for each insight, and the prioritized recommendations. At this point in the prototyping process, it's best to present these findings to your full team, including product manager, development team, and business stakeholders. Research findings are helpful to all areas of the product team, and the more involved they are in the insights and recommendations, the better buy-in you will have when you want to move in a certain direction.

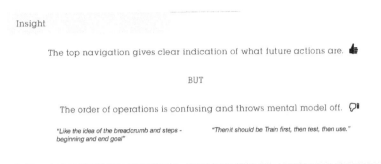

Insight

The top navigation gives clear indication of what future actions are. 👍

BUT

The order of operations is confusing and throws mental model off. 💬

"Like the idea of the breadcrumb and steps - beginning and end goal"

"Then it should be Train first, then test, then use."

Recommendation

- Replace 'use' with 'Try Out'
- Consider rearranging the order of operations

FIGURE 7-8

You can present insights as an opportunity area to improve

This testing process will help you improve your product, communicate those improvements to your stakeholders, and keep the user central to your design. With a little bit of planning, you can conduct these experiments as part of your weekly or biweekly sprint cycle or longer-term workflow (for more about Agile workflows, see the sidebar in Chapter 1).

Summary

Testing prototypes with users helps you discover what works and doesn't work with your current idea. It's a great way to get specific feedback on how your ideal user would interact with your product. You need to create a research plan to guide the session, and carefully craft the questions and tasks you will have the user do during the test.

During the research session, make sure to have a second person to take notes, record the session, and get the user to talk openly about what they're thinking. The most mundane reaction may lead to the most insightful improvement, so keep an eye out for microexpressions and interesting uses or navigations. After you've run enough tests, synthesize your findings to discover the insights that will improve your product. Use these insights to create recommendations and communicate them to your team before improving the next prototype, and you're on your way to incremental improvements!

[8]

Pulling It All Together—
SXSW Tasting Experience

THIS CASE STUDY SHOWS the combination of prototyping for both physical and digital interactions in one experience. The IBM Mobile Innovation Lab (MIL) explores how emerging technology can combine with IBM's enterprise-level cloud, IoT, and development platforms. They take on and invent innovation projects that will push the entire business unit and company forward, and are often the first team to try new technologies in application to enterprise.

For the 2016 South by Southwest conference (SXSW), the MIL was challenged to create an exciting experience for the conference attendees that showcased the lab's design capabilities and machine learning skills (Figure 8-1). The users the team designed for were mostly from out of town; were visiting Austin, Texas for the first time; worked for tech companies or startups or were part of the design community; and were interested in experiencing the authentic Austin.

The design and development team knew that they wanted to blend physical and digital aspects to create an all-encompassing experience for their users, and that they were constrained by needing to deal with large crowds and a loud environment. They had only five weeks to design, build, and test the entire experience, so they had to move fast and jump straight into making.

FIGURE 8-1

The MIL created an interactive experience for SXSW with a user-centered, iterative process

Originally, they wanted to create an experience where the user could learn about Austin and which neighborhoods or sites to see based on the user's interests. The team would tie into the travel aspect of the conference, and how it brings people from all over the world to Austin. After assessing the timeline and what they could accomplish in five weeks in addition to researching the users' interests, they adjusted the scope, and decided that exposing the crowd to the Austin craft beer scene would be an ideal experience. They wanted to match users with a local beer based on their tastes and preferences.

Research

The first step to build out this experience was to gather as much data as possible on their users and beer tastes so that the team could connect food, beverage, and seasonal preferences to types of beer. The user research team, Aide Gutierrez-Gonzalez and Becca Shuman, created a survey and did in-person interviews and card sorts, gathering around 430 individual responses to build their ground truth for beer taste preferences (Figure 8-2). *Ground truth* is the foundational information used to train a machine-learning algorithm. The quality of this data directly affects the quality of the output the algorithm will give. The team built out a recommendation engine based on the research to give accurate results that would improve over time through machine learning techniques. The team reached out to businesses for additional research and support. Whichcraft, a local beer store with a huge selection and expert staff, provided baseline data about how they recommend new beers to customers.

FIGURE 8-2
Aide Gutierrez-Gonzalez and Becca Shuman conducted card sorts with users

User Flow

Based on the initial research, the team created a user flow diagram to help communicate the different touchpoints of the experience (Figure 8-3). The user first answers a series of questions about food preferences, which the barkeeper facilitator inputs into an iPad interface. Based on those answers, the recommendation engine algorithm suggests three different beers, which the barkeep pours for the user. The user tastes those three beers blindly, and arranges them on the table from most to least favorite. While they taste the beers, anonymized information about each beer is shown on a large display screen, triggered by the specific beer cups. When the user chooses their favorite, the display reveals which beer was selected and additional information about that beer. The user's preference is then saved to the engine's database to improve its recommendation for future users.

FIGURE 8-3

The team created a user flow to understand and scope the entire experience

The Physical Side

The development team researched different physical interfaces and the technology they would need to have the cups and beer types visually recognized to create a seamless experience. The team knew that they wanted a physical table and beer cups to be the main interaction for the user, instead of having the user touch a screen. This motion and movement are a natural part of lifting and tasting from cups, so the team wanted the arrangement of the cups to be part of the final ranking system for the user.

The team started by evaluating RFID sensors and tags to see if they could get the necessary cup information without requiring specific actions from the users (Figure 8-4). Based on quick tests, they discovered that RFID sensors had too small of a receiving area, and required exact placement by the user, which was not ideal.

FIGURE 8-4

An initial exploration used RFID sensors to trigger specific outputs

Next, they tried out a visual recognition application using a camera. The team color-coded their cup bottoms and placed them on an acrylic tabletop (Figure 8-5). Through testing, they realized they needed more clarity than just the different colors, so they tried QR codes instead. The combination of QR codes and camera recognition worked well, and they moved on to testing how the users interacted with ordering and rating their preferred beer (Figure 8-6).

FIGURE 8-5
Tabletop testing of cups

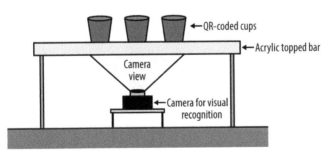

FIGURE 8-6
Diagram of visual recognition setup

The Digital Side

At this point, the development and research side of the team was well on their way to having a solid ground truth and interactive surface. So the designers began creating the barkeepers' digital interface and the displays for the data visualizations and unique beer information. They first created the barkeeper's tablet application that displays a series of questions and allows the barkeeper to input the user's choice (Figure 8-7). Because it was a simple survey, the designers were able to jump straight into mid-fidelity wireframes and building a clickable prototype to test. It had to be easy to read and fast in reaction to keep the experience flowing, so these were key parts of the testing they conducted.

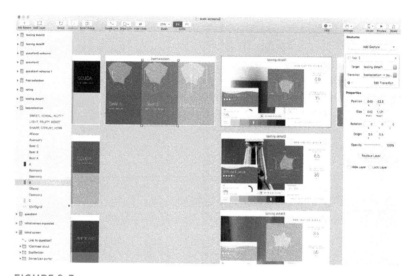

FIGURE 8-7
The designers created wireframes for the barkeeper's interface

For the data visualization display, the designers realized the interface would need to include animations and transitions in order to create a seamless, immersive experience. They designed how the data displayed and flowed between the initial test and tasting, and between each anonymous beer. Knowing that the animations would take quite a bit of development time to implement, the team very quickly moved from static wireframes in Illustrator to dynamic prototypes using both Sketch and Flinto to test and refine their designs (Figures 8-8 and 8-9).

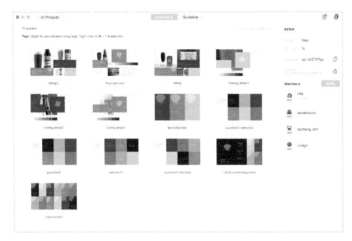

FIGURE 8-8

The designers created data visualizations in Sketch and Flinto

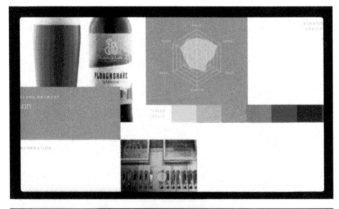

FIGURE 8-9

They tested the animations on large televisions equipped with Apple TVs

The design team's main process for prototyping and communicating screen design was drawing mid- to high-fidelity wireframes in Sketch, and then using Flinto to create prototypes and motion-based studies. They exported the files into Zeplin, a plug-in that automatically creates a style guide and redlines for the design, so that developers have all the information they need to implement the work.

The last major aspect of the experience that the team prototyped and tested individually was the rating system (Figure 8-10). Each team member had their own mental model of how to rate the three anonymous beers that did not align. They got stuck trying to figure out the best way to rank the beers. Do they use smiley-face emojis, hearts, or stars? Or should they create a more complex matrix so that they could collect more rigorous data points to improve their machine learning model? The best way to make a decision for the interface was to test the different variations with users.

FIGURE 8-10

The team created many different ways to rate the beers, the first being a matrix

They conducted A/B tests with stars and hearts, having the user do two rounds of organizing, one with each option (Figure 8-11). They switched the order of which icon came first in the test, in order to balance out the findings.

FIGURE 8-11
The user research team conducted A/B testing to inform their rating system

Based on the research, the star rating system turned out to be the more intuitive of the two options. It was the best way for users to organize their beers, while still having them land in the proper area for the QR code camera to see. With the rating system in place, the technology working for the object recognition, and the barkeeper interface and animated visualizations, the team was ready to test the entire experience together.

Bringing It Together

The team knew that the physical environment would provide a lot of context to the survey and rating interactions, so they built a bar with a large television display and an acrylic top to user test together (Figure 8-12). They CNC-milled plywood covers for the TV stands, and spent hours sanding, painting, and finishing the displays and tables. They then printed or drew paper versions of the vinyl tabletop designs of the rating system and cup zones. By using paper, they could quickly change the design or pivot based on testing results. They conducted the rating system A/B testing with paper too. Later in the process, they printed high-fidelity vinyl stickers to ensure that they were understood.

FIGURE 8-12
The team created a full environment for the interaction and display

The team wrote out a script for the barkeepers and practiced the fine-tooth details—like transitions between the different parts of the experience and the setup of the environment to make it easy to pour the three tasting beers (Figure 8-13). The practice really paid off in the smooth execution of the experience (Figure 8-14).

FIGURE 8-13
The testing and design really paid off at the final setup

FIGURE 8-14
The experience was executed smoothly with great results

The Final Experience

The final Tasting Experience was a huge hit at the SXSW conference (Figure 8-15). The team completed 167 individual beer consultations and poured more than 500 beers to taste. Aide Gutierrez-Gonzalez says the most successful part of the design process was how well design, development, and research collaborated together to test and complete the project. The close collaboration allowed them to move quickly with impressive results. They were able to make sure the experience made sense and was enjoyable for real people, not merely for designers or developers.

FIGURE 8-15

The final Taste experience was a huge success; the lines were long, waiting to try out the experience.

Summary

Because of the success at SXSW, the MIL team is working on new applications of this experience in the retail area. They have three different scales that they are developing further: a suitcase version that can be displayed at meetings and meetups, a pop-up shop version to take to events and conferences, and a permanent kiosk version that can live in a store and give users recommendations on all sorts of purchases (Figure 8-16). This entire experience is actually a prototype of a smart shelf concept that would seamlessly blend into a shopping environment, but give users extra context into personalized recommendations.

The team successfully tested their assumptions and used the direct feedback to improve their Tasting Experience. By dividing and conquering the physical and digital sides simultaneously, the team covered more ground and was able to test more assumptions. This testing allowed them to deliver a robust, immersive experience with only five weeks of work.

FIGURE 8-16

The team has since expanded the concept into different scales and use cases

The MIL's success shows that a team culture of prototyping and testing ideas helps to create immersive products and experiences that really solve user needs. It allowed them to collaborate more closely with all parts of the team (including developers, product owners, and designers) and to align on real, grounded reasons for their design decisions.

[9]

What Have We Learned

Now THAT WE'VE REACHED the end of this book, you should be inspired and empowered to create prototypes for your work. You're on your way to developing a thirst for prototyping and testing your ideas, in all areas of your work and life. You'll begin to see yourself testing ideas at a low-fidelity level, and consciously learning and improving them. You might notice yourself reframing design requirements at work into user-centered challenges. Instead of "I need this widget to export data reports," you'll think "how can I make the most intuitive data reporting interface for my user?" You might even start hacking fun electronic projects to try in your home—like an automatic light color changer, or a doorbell that tweets whenever someone rings.

FIGURE 9-1
Each day is a prototype that you can improve on tomorrow, designed and printed by Patrick Chew

Hopefully you've learned a ton and now feel capable of building the right prototype for your situation. You now have a strong foundational understanding of what needs to be prototyped and the process of prototyping. You can choose the software you'd like to learn, and apply this new knowledge to framing and scoping the prototypes you build.

If you haven't yet tried it, go grab a stack of Post-its and take a minute to draw out a new app idea or device interface as a paper prototype. Or write out a user flow for that new smart object you've been considering building. Let this book inspire you to take action and make visible the ideas that are in your head. When we invent new products that solve a real user problem, we're improving the world. Figure out how you can contribute to that better world, and get making!

[*Appendix A*]

Resources and Links

Sources for Tutorials and Learning

- Adafruit (*https://learn.adafruit.com*)

- AngularJS (*angularjs.org*)

- Arduino official tutorials (*http://bit.ly/2gNp7Ek*)

- Basic electronics Instructable (*http://bit.ly/2gQYdvm*)

- Bento Front End tracks (*https://bento.io/tracks*) offers free full stack web development training curated from all the best resources online through videos and links to tutorials.

- Bootstrap (*getbootstrap.com*)

- Codeacademy (*https://www.codecademy.com*) has many coding courses with side-by-side instruction, code, and display so you can learn and see what you're coding immediately.

- Codepen (*http://codepen.io*) is a free sandbox environment with side-by-side HTML, CSS, JavaScript, and display panes, and a community with tons of open source code and animations that you can riff off of.

- Electronics learning series from SparkFun (*http://bit.ly/2gPGuo4*)

- Fritzing (*http://fritzing.org/home/*)

- Instructables (*http://www.instructables.com*)

- Lynda (*https://www.lynda.com*) is a paid subscription to extensive library of training videos for not only coding, but also design and business.

- Makezine: (*http://makezine.com*)

- Soldering tutorial (*http://bit.ly/2gPEbkK*)

- Sparkfun (*http://learn.sparkfun.com/tutorials*)

- Treehouse (*https://teamtreehouse.com*) is a paid subscription to over 1,000 videos, quizzes, and code challenges.

- Usability.gov (*http://www.usability.gov*)

- Usability.gov's consent form (*http://bit.ly/2gQP0mR*)

- Usability.gov's research template (*http://bit.ly/2gPHWGK*)

- UserTesting.com for remote user testing (*usertesting.com*)

Sources for Materials

- Adafruit (*https://www.adafruit.com*)

- AliExpress (*http://bit.ly/2gPCd3K*)

- All Electronics (*http://www.allelectronics.com*)

- Arduino Pro Mini (*https://www.sparkfun.com/products/11114*)

- Arduino Starter Kit (*http://bit.ly/2gPzQOI*)

- Bluetooth starter kit (*https://www.adafruit.com/products/3026*)

- Full soldering setup (*http://www.adafruit.com/products/136*)

- Jameco (*http://www.jameco.com*)

- LightBlue Bean (Bluetooth microcontroller) (*http://bit.ly/2hMhWg8*)

- littleBits (*http://littlebits.cc*)

- OSH Park PCBs (*https://oshpark.com*)

- Makershed (*http://www.makershed.com*)

- Motor kit (*https://www.adafruit.com/products/171*)

- Particle WiFi and cellular microcontrollers (*https://www.particle.io*)

- Rainbow pack of LEDs (*http://bit.ly/2gPEBrr*)

- Robot kit (*https://www.adafruit.com/products/749*)

- Sensor pack (*https://www.adafruit.com/products/176*)

- SparkFun (*https://www.sparkfun.com*)

- Trinket (*https://www.adafruit.com/products/1500*)

- WiFi starter kit (*https://www.adafruit.com/products/2680*)

Recommended Books and Articles

- *12 Best Practices for UX in Agile* (*https://articles.uie.com/best_practices/* and *https://articles.uie.com/best_practices_part2/*)

- *Arduino Cookbook* by Michael Margolis (O'Reilly)

- *Arduino in a Nutshell* (O'Reilly)

- Contrast Ratio Tool from Lea Verou (*http://leaverou.github.io/contrast-ratio/*)

- *Designing for Touch* by Josh Clark (A Book Apart)

- *Designing for Performance* by Lara Hogan (O'Reilly)

- *Designing Interface Animation* by Val Head (Rosenfeld Media)

- "Doing UX in an Agile World" (*https://www.nngroup.com/articles/doing-ux-agile-world/*)

- Email notifier project (*http://bit.ly/2gPEpsd*)

- *How to Make Sense of Any Mess* by Abby Covert (Createspace Independent Publishing)

- *Information Architecture for the World Wide Web* by Peter Morville and Louise Rosenfeld

- *Just Enough Research* by Erika Hall (A Book Apart)

- *Gamestorming* by Dave Gray, Sunni Brown, and James Macanufo (O'Reilly)

- Intro to Sass (*http://bit.ly/2gPxKyf*)

- Keynote animations Smashing Mag (*http://bit.ly/2gPCF1W*)

- *Lean Business Canvas* (LeanStack)

- *Lean Startup* series (O'Reilly)

- *Make: Electronics* by Charles Platt (Maker Media)

- *Making It: Manufacturing Techniques for Product Design* by Chris Lefteri (Central Saint Martins College)

- *Materials and Design* by Mike Ashby and Kara Johnson (Elsevier)

- *Materials for Design* by Chris Lefteri (Laurence King Publishing)

- *Mechanical Engineering for Hackers* by Will McLeod (O'Reilly)

- *Mobile First* by Luke Wroblewski (A Book Apart)

- "Persona Empathy Mapping" by Cooper (*http://bit.ly/2gPAT14*)

- *Programming Arduino: Getting Started with Sketches* by Simon Monk (McGraw-Hill)

- *Prototype to Product: A Practical Guide for Getting to Market* by Alan Cohen (O'Reilly)

- Prototyping tools by Emily Schwartzman and Cooper (*https://www.cooper.com/prototyping-tools*)

- *Responsive Web Design* by Ethan Marcotte (O'Reilly)

- RGB LED code library (*http://bit.ly/2gPDsA8*)

- *Running Lean* by Ash Maurya (O'Reilly)

- UX for the Masses, "A step by step guide to scenario mapping" (*http://bit.ly/2gPEMmB*)

- *UX Strategy* by Jaime Levy (O'Reilly)

- Walkthrough of an Arduino sketch file (*http://bit.ly/2gPE7l2*)

- Web Accessibility Toolkit (*http://bit.ly/2gPEhZu*)

Image Citations

- Figure P-1: "Rachel Kalmar's datapunk quantified self sensor array 2," (*http://bit.ly/2hi5ruv*) by Doctorow (*http://bit.ly/2hiik7X*) is licensed under CC BY 2.0 (*https://creativecommons.org/licenses/by-sa/2.0/*).

- Figure P-2: "JavaScript UI widgets library" (*http://bit.ly/2hicBPy*), by Kelluvuus is licensed under CC BY 4.0 (*https://creativecommons.org/licenses/by-sa/4.0/deed.en*).

- Figure 1-2: "F * R * I * E * N * D * S ~ Central Perk Café" (*http://bit.ly/2hidgAr*) by prayitnophotography (*https://www.flickr.com/photos/prayitnophotography/*) is licensed under CC BY 2.0 (*https://creativecommons.org/licenses/by/2.0/*).

- Figure 1-4: "IMG_8871 - 2013-0518" (*http://bit.ly/2himQDs*) by eager (*https://www.flickr.com/photos/eager/*) is licensed under CC BY 2.0 (*https://creativecommons.org/licenses/by/2.0/*).

- Figure 1-5: "OXO Good Grips Swivel Peeler" (*https://www.oxo.com/swivel-peeler-241*) by Oxo.

- Figure 1-6: "Aston Martin Shoe Sketch" (*http://bit.ly/2hil1WT*) by Kirby (*http://bit.ly/2higELM*) is licensed under CC BY 2.0 (*https://creativecommons.org/licenses/by-nd/2.0/*).

- Figure 1-9: "App sketching" (*http://bit.ly/2hi9AhU*) by Johan Larsson (*https://www.flickr.com/photos/johanl/*) is licensed under CC BY 2.0 (*https://creativecommons.org/licenses/by/2.0/*).

- Figure 1-12: "Ray und Charles Eames: Beinschiene, Modell S2-1790. 1941" (*http://bit.ly/2hidR59*) by René Spitz is licensed under CC BY-ND 2.0 (*https://creativecommons.org/licenses/by-nd/2.0/*) and "LCW (Lounge Chair D22:E22)" (*http://bit.ly/2hspK8O*) by Hiart is licensed under public domain.

- Figure 2-5: "Business Model Canvas" (*http://bit.ly/2higX9o*) by Business Model Alchemist is licensed under CC BY 1.0 (*https://creativecommons.org/licenses/by-sa/1.0/deed.en*).

- Figure 3-2: "Essai circuit préAmp (TDA2003) 1:1048576 (*http://bit.ly/2hsrK0J*) by Dileck (*http://bit.ly/2hseXey*) is licensed under CC BY-SA 2.0 (*https://creativecommons.org/licenses/by-sa/2.0/*).

- Figure 3-9: "Let me show you Mah Ponk..." (*http://bit.ly/2hsi8CW*) by svofski (*https://www.flickr.com/photos/svofski/*) is licensed under CC BY 2.0 (*https://creativecommons.org/licenses/by/2.0/*).

- Figure 4-5: "Setting up your Nest" (*http://bit.ly/2hi6H0H*) by Android Central.

- Figure 4-15: "Bodystorming" (*http://bit.ly/2hi8IKh*) by Unsworn Industries is licensed under CC BY-SA 2.0 (*https://creativecommons.org/licenses/by-sa/2.0/*).

- Figure 4-29: Etsy shop "Fell From Corvidia" (*https://www.etsy.com/shop/fellfromcorvidia*).

- Figure 5-7: "Mobile First" (*http://bit.ly/2hia33E*) by Brad Frost.

- Figure 5-9: "Android Fragmentation Visualized" (*http://bit.ly/2hignrS*).

- Figure 5-11: "paper-prototype" (*http://bit.ly/2hihnfY*) by Rob Enslin is licensed under CC BY 2.0 (*https://creativecommons.org/licenses/by/2.0/*).

- Figure 5-14: "Types of colorblindness" (*http://bit.ly/2gQYfTW*).

- Figure 5-26: "Projects Paper-based Prototyping and Functional Testing Part" (*http://bit.ly/2hik94N*) by Samuel Mann is licensed under CC BY 2.0 (*https://creativecommons.org/licenses/by/2.0/*).

- Figure 5-29: "b.ook - wireframes" (*http://bit.ly/2hiaJGg*) by andreas.trianta is licensed under CC BY 2.0 (*https://creativecommons.org/licenses/by/2.0/*).

- Figure 5-31: "Wireframing Template Sketch resource" (*http://bit.ly/2hiopBk*) is licensed under CC BY (*https://creativecommons.org/licenses/by/2.0/*).

- Figure 5-32: "Move Mobile UI kit" (*http://bit.ly/2hilgRI*) by Kurbatov Volodymyr (*https://gumroad.com/coob*).

- Figure 5-35: "eDidaktikum" (*http://bit.ly/2hioFjM*) by Priit Tammets is licensed under CC BY 2.0 (*https://creativecommons.org/licenses/by/2.0/*).

- Figure 5-46: "The Sass syntax" (*http://bit.ly/2hif10A*) by smashingbuzz.

- Figure 5-61: "Cedar Point sky-view" (*http://bit.ly/2hicl2Y*) by David Fulmer is licensed under CC BY 2.0 (*https://creativecommons.org/licenses/by/2.0/*).

- Figure 5-62: "beacons by jnxyz.education" (*http://bit.ly/2hipB7x*) by Jona Nalder is licensed under CC BY 2.0 (*https://creativecommons.org/licenses/by/2.0/*).

- Figure 6-4: "_WRK3525" (*http://bit.ly/2hsp3MJ*) by Intel Free Press (*https://www.flickr.com/photos/intelfreepress/*) is licensed under CC BY-SA 2.0 (*https://creativecommons.org/licenses/by-sa/2.0/*).

- Figure 6-7: "Arduino Uno" (*http://bit.ly/2hiqvB6*) by Dllu is licensed under CC BY-SA 4.0 (*https://creativecommons.org/licenses/by-sa/4.0/deed.en*).

- Figure 6-9: "Wearable technology for the wrist" (*http://bit.ly/2hik-pAw*) by Intel Free Press is licensed under CC BY-SA 2.0 (*https://creativecommons.org/licenses/by-sa/2.0/*).

- Figure 6-10: "Misfit Shine" (*http://bit.ly/2hinXTD*).

- Figure 6-13: "Examples of momentary switches" (*http://bit.ly/2hi-lyIG*) by Jimbo at SparkFun.

- Figure 6-20: "Protoboard Unitec" (*http://bit.ly/2hijO1Y*) by Victoria. nunez2 is licensed under CC BY-SA 4.0 (*https://creativecommons.org/licenses/by-sa/4.0/deed.en*).

- Figure 6-52: Rough Prototype by IDEO (*https://labs.ideo.com/about/*).

- Figure 6-53: Olympus PK diego Powered Debrider System (*http://bit.ly/2hsmpXh*).

- Figure 6-55: "Solderedjoint" (*http://bit.ly/2hieLym*) by MJN123 is licensed under CC BY 3.0 (*https://creativecommons.org/licenses/by/3.0/*).

- Figure 6-56: "Lochplatinen" (*http://bit.ly/2hiplp0*) by PeterFrankfurt is licensed under public domain and "PCB" (*http://bit.ly/2hskEt3*) by MichaelFrey is licensed CC BY-SA 2.0 DE (*https://creativecommons.org/licenses/by-sa/2.0/de/deed.en*).

- Figure 6-60: "MINIFIGURE ATMEL SAMD21 BOARD" (*http://bit.ly/2hJcl97*) by Benjamin Shockley.

- Figure 6-61: "Soldering a 0805" (*http://bit.ly/2hipEQN*) by Aisart is licensed under CC BY-SA 3.0 (*https://creativecommons.org/licenses/by-sa/3.0/deed.en*).

- Figure 6-62: "3D printing at home" (*http://bit.ly/2hitsS3*) by La Tarte au Citron is licensed under CC BY-ND 2.0 (*https://creativecommons.org/licenses/by-nd/2.0/*).

- Figure 7-4: "7 universal facial expressions of emotions" (*http://bit.ly/2hiiqfF*) by Icerko Lydia is licensed under CC BY 3.0 (*https://creativecommons.org/licenses/by/3.0/deed.en*).

Glossary

Adafruit (https://www.adafruit.com)
> Electronics company that sells components and kits for all sorts of electronics projects

Affinity mapping
> A way to organize data by grouping it based on natural relationships or similar topics

Agile
> A project management methodology of continuous delivery, planning, integration, and radical team collaboration

As-is scenario
> A journey map that goes step by step through the user's current experience of a product, and states what the user is doing, thinking, and feeling throughout each step of that process

Assumption
> A belief or feeling that something is true or that something will happen, although there is no proof

Beacons
> Small, Bluetooth-based sensors that send contextual information or directions to smartphones when they are in proximity to the sensor

Bodystorming
> A performance-based ideation where your team role-plays the specific users and situations to understand how that user currently deals with their problems and how they might interact and react to your new ideas

Code framework

A hierarchical directory that encapsulates shared resources, such as a dynamic shared library, nib files, image files, localized strings, header files, and reference documentation in a single package (some examples include Bootstrap, AngularJS, or Foundation)

Contextual inquiry

A research method where a researcher observes a user in their own environment doing normal activities and asks follow-up questions about why the user completes tasks in a certain way

Empathy map

A collaborative tool for teams to gain empathy and a deeper understanding of their user by exploring what they think, feel, do, and say

Fidelity

How closely a prototype or experience resembles the final product in the dimensions of visual, breadth, depth, interactivity, and data model

Fritzing (http://fritzing.org/home/)

An open source tool to digitally design, create, and test circuits or PCBs

Ground truth

The foundational information used to train a machine learning algorithm

Hamburger menu

A button consisting of three parallel horizontal lines that typically hides a menu of pages or navigation options

Honorarium

A payment given to a person who gives time in a volunteer capacity or for services for which fees are not traditionally required

Information architecture (IA)

The structural design, labeling, and organization of shared information environments such as software and websites

Intercept interview

A short, on-site interview where users are approached as they are going about their own business

Lean Business Canvas

An adaptation of the Business Model Canvas that helps you build a business model by understanding your product and the market it will sell in

littleBits (http://littlebits.cc)

Electronics company that sells easy-to-use, magnetic component blocks for kids of all ages

Lorem ipsum

Filler text commonly used to lay out screen designs before real content is available

Maker Faire

A festival celebrating the maker movement by gathering the enthusiastic DIYers, technologers, and hobbyists

Mental model

An individual's thought process about how something works in the real world

Microexpression

A brief, involuntary facial expression shown on the face of humans according to emotions experienced

Minimum viable product (MVP)

A product with just enough features to deliver to market, test, and gather validated learnings about how to continue development

Minimum viable prototype

A generalized approach to prototyping, using the least amount of effort to test a specific assumption or to physicalize an idea

Multimeter

An instrument that measures electric current, voltage, and resistance over several ranges of value

Pain point

A real or perceived problem that a user has with current or new products or experiences

Pattern Library

A collection of user interface design patterns that consists of visually designed components in software like Sketch or Illustrator, and coded components for developers

PCB

Printed circuit boards are custom boards with specific components and circuits already embedded or etched into the finished surface

Perfboard

A thin, rigid sheet for prototyping electronic circuits with predrilled holes and copper pads to make it easy to solder components onto it

Performance

The speed that a web page downloads and displays when a user loads it

Persona

A summary about a specific type of user based on research and observation, used for communication and to keep the team focused on the specific goals of their user throughout the design process

Product roadmap

An alignment tool that describes how a product will likely grow over a specific period of time, including future features that will be implemented

Product strategy

Includes a vision, goals, and initiatives for a new product in order to align and inspire the team towards a specific direction for the product

Proof of concept (POC)

A demonstration of a product idea or theory designed to determine feasibility and market impact

Protoboard

The generalized term for a prototyping board that allows you to solder a circuit in a more robust way; the two most common types are perfboard and stripboard

Prototype

A manifestation of an idea into a format that communicates the idea to others or is tested with users, with the intention to improve that idea over time

Redlines

A communication tool where annotations are added to design deliverables to specify dimensions, colors, and interactions so that developers can easily implement the designs

Retrospective

A meeting held after an Agile sprint to reflect on the work that was completed by determining what went well and what could be improved for future sprints

Roadmap

A document that describes the next six months to one year of work on a product in small, prioritized chunks

Schematic

A representation of the elements in an electronic circuit using abstract graphic symbols rather than realistic pictures

Scope

The extent of the area or subject matter that something deals with or to which it is relevant

Short circuit

An electrical circuit that allows a current to travel on an unintended path with very little resistance that often results in blown out components or unintended problems

SparkFun (https://www.sparkfun.com)

An online retail store that sells electronic components and kits

Sprint

In Agile, a sprint is a timeboxed effort that is planned with a specific outcome in mind; it can be anywhere from one week to one month, with two weeks being a common length

Stand-up

A daily status meeting in Agile where a team meets and describes what each person accomplished the previous day and what they will work on that day

Sticky navigation (also persistent navigation)

A navigation bar that remains fixed to the top of a browser so that when the user scrolls, it remains accessible

Stripboard

A protoboard that has parallel strips of copper running in one direction to allow for easy soldering of circuits

User flow

The path a user follows through a product in order to complete a task or goal

User-centered design (UCD)

The process of designing a product from the perspective of how it will be understood and used by a human user rather than requiring users to adapt their attitudes and behaviors in order to learn and use a system

Wireframe

A skeletal framework or page layout of a digital product that can be created at a low or high fidelity based on the goal of the wireframe

Z-index

A CSS attribute that specifies the order of the layering of objects when rendering content for digital products

[*Index*]

About the Author

Kathryn McElroy is a Designer at the IBM Mobile Innovation Lab in Austin, Texas. She is an award-winning designer and photographer and is passionate about near-future technology, artificial intelligence, smart objects, and open hardware and software. She has published tutorials and articles about her projects in *Make: Magazine, Fast Company, Timeout New York,* and in multiple books including *Make: The Best of, Volume 2* and *Making Simple Robots.* Kathryn regularly speaks about design thinking, prototyping, and user experience design, and her passion is teaching people how easy it is to get started making with electronics.

Colophon

The animal on the cover of *Prototyping for Designers* is an Australasian swamphen (*Porphyrio melanotus*), known as a pukeko in the Maori language. These birds are found on mainland Australia, Indonesia, the Moluccas, Aru, and Kai Islands, and Papua New Guinea.

Swamphens that live in New Zealand are generally larger than those on mainland Australia.

Swamphens are clumsy upon takeoff and landing, and so often respond to being threatened by walking away rather than flying. They live in groups of 3–12, and are known to shriek loudly to defend their nests from Australasian harrier attacks. If unsuccessful at warding off predators, they may abandon the nest altogether.

Because of its reddish face, beak, and legs, the swamphen is revered in many island cultures such as the Maori in New Zealand and in Samoa, where the color red is associated with nobility and power. It's also present in Maori mythology and metaphor: a person who is considered a pukeko is stubborn and annoying, much like the swamphens that raid gardens for sweet potato and taro.

In New Zealand, swamphens are protected as native gamebirds and can be hunted only under license. However, they are not considered good food; their meat is sinewy and tough.

Many of the animals on O'Reilly covers are endangered; all of them are important to the world. To learn more about how you can help, go to *animals.oreilly.com*.

Learn from experts.
Find the answers you need.

Sign up for a **10-day free trial** to get **unlimited access** to all of the content on Safari, including Learning Paths, interactive tutorials, and curated playlists that draw from thousands of ebooks and training videos on a wide range of topics, including data, design, DevOps, management, business—and much more.

Start your free trial at:
oreilly.com/safari

(No credit card required.)